Bee Wise

Bee Wise

12 LEADERSHIP LESSONS
FROM A BUSY BEEHIVE

PHILIP ATKINSON

&

GUEST WRITERS

BuzzWorks Publishing
Switzerland

Published by BuzzWorks Publishing
An imprint of Hive Communications Group, GmbH
Bernoullistrasse 20
Basel, 4056 Switzerland
Hive-Logic.com
Philip@Hive-Logic.com

BuzzWorks books are available at special quantity discounts when purchased in bulk for sales promotions, premiums, fundraising and educational needs. Special books or book excerpts can also be created to fit specific needs. For details and permission requests, write to the email address above.

The author and publisher have made every reasonable effort to obtain the necessary permissions for the use of copyrighted material. In the event of any inadvertent errors or omissions, the publisher will address and correct them in subsequent editions of the book.

Neither the author nor the publisher shall be liable or responsible for any loss or damage allegedly arising from any information or suggestion in this book.

ISBN 978-3-9526140-0-6 (hardback)
ISBN 978-3-9526140-1-3 (paperback)
ISBN 978-3-9526140-2-0 (eBook)

10 9 8 7 6 5 4 3 2 1

—

Copyediting by Joanna Puckering
Proofreading by Adeline Hull
Cover Art & Illustrations by Maria Malecha
Author Photo by Howard Brundrett
Book Design & Publishing by Kory Kirby
SET IN BASKERVILLE URW

This book is dedicated to my dear Grandad, Tom Dennis, who was a great nature lover and storyteller. And a great supporter of my random acts of enthusiasm.

Bees for Development

An important goal for this book project is to raise awareness and vital funds for the charity, Bees for Development. They work tirelessly to support communities in developing countries to make and sell honey as a sustainable business. Your purchase of this book will help us to continue to support their work.

www.BeesforDevelopment.org

Contents

Introduction

The beehive is the ultimate business case study for complex organisations and working life today. Through learning about the bees and what happens inside a hard-working hive we will gain a fresh perspective on the most pressing challenges facing leaders and every organisation today.

ON A COOL MAY MORNING IN 2019, I found myself standing on the giant wing of a Boeing 737.

Dressed in my beekeeper's suit.

Carrying an empty cardboard box.

A nervous crowd of pilots, mechanics and security people in yellow jackets were all watching this bizarre scene.

Earlier, I had received an urgent call from my local airport; a swarm of bees had attached themselves to the crevice between the wing and the fuselage of a plane at Basel Airport. The pilot was refusing to take off until they had been cleared.

Could I help?

Hell, yes.

With great excitement – and some apprehension – I drove to the airport, gained security clearance to drive directly onto the runway, and positioned my car underneath the wing of this plane. Then I climbed into a cherry picker that lifted me high into the air so I could tentatively climb onto the wing.

Walking in a heavy bee suit is not easy. Walking along the wing of a 737, even less so. You're a little more clumsy, and with reduced visibility, with all eyes on you – it's terrifying. One wrong step and you're looking at a rather painful drop onto the tarmac.

But despite that, I thought, *this is the most exciting day of my life.*

When I found the culprits, they were huddled together for warmth. They had set off as a swarm the night before when it had been warm and sunny, and the metal of the fuselage must have seemed a safe and cosy spot to rest. Now, the sun was on the other side; they were in the shade and it was too cold for them to fly. Carefully, and with all eyes watching, I slowly scooped the 30,000 or so bees off the plane and into a cardboard box. I checked the queen was safe and carried the swarm out of harm's way. It must have been quite a sight for anyone unaware of the situation: a man dressed as a beekeeper fussing around the wing of a 737.

I then had to quickly change from wearing my bee suit to a business suit, and go to my own place of work – a large multinational corporation.

As I arrived at the office, I watched people walk in and out of this building through a small main door, some carrying briefcases, full of ideas and experiences, others wearing expressions of concentration or engaged in conversation. I happened to know this was a building where people developed medicines and life-saving cancer treatments, but you wouldn't be able to tell just by watching.

As workers hovered outside and waited for the bus to go to the airport or to meet friends, I slowly realised the building looked and sounded a bit like a beehive. There was a reception area just like the landing pad of a hive, and inside the building were lifts and escalators to different floors and corridors to different rooms. There was a real buzz – an active noise – and each worker had their role and their place within the complex system.

Having noticed the metaphor of beekeeping and the workings of a large organisation, I saw the connections everywhere. It was impossible to avoid the parallels between the two. My curiosity was piqued.

It's easy to walk past a small group of bees and not think much about them – just as it's easy to avoid thinking about how we lead and how we work. But every single meeting, every workshop, every client and every project has parallels between hardworking bees and hard-working people and companies. The first time you take the lid off your own real-life beehive (in my case, literal and metaphorical), no matter how much theory you've read and no matter how much you watch on YouTube, it's absolutely terrifying.

You've no idea what's going on.

It doesn't make any sense, and it doesn't look like it does in the textbooks.

It's overwhelming – and then the buggers try and sting you.

So, let's lift the lid on the intimate and intricate workings of honey bees and their hives and use them as a starting point to think more about our situation in businesses, in teams, as leaders and members of society. For me, it's a fun metaphor that's grown and grown and now forms part of our identity at the company I founded – Hive-Logic Coaching & Communications – and the work we do.

We could all benefit from thinking more about these things: about our place in the world and our place as leaders in work. We are all role models – parents, family members and members of society – and we all have a responsibility to be more conscious and think about how we impact others.

How This Book Is Structured

This book is for anyone curious about their role at work today and in the future. You may currently be working in a large organisation. Or leaving one. You may be struggling with the current pace of change or feeling threatened by exposure to new technologies and new competitors. You may be self-employed and working hard to grow a business. You may be considering further education or at a point in your career when you're wondering what is next.

This book leads us, through the fascinating metaphor of a hard-working beehive, to twelve key topics relevant to leadership today. At the end of each chapter, I have invited a trusted colleague to respond with their own lived experience and thoughts about working with organisations as a leader, coach or consultant. This approach to collaboration and teamwork is highly compatible with how I like to work, but it seems to be rarely done in books today. Let's hope it sets a precedent for future work.

Cycles of beginnings, middles and endings are very important in life and in work. This book is structured across the annual cycle of beekeeping, with four sections – Spring, Summer, Autumn and Winter – each divided into three chapters. This closely reflects bees' progression through the year and that of the beekeeper trying to catch up. Business life also has its own natural cycles that we need to be aware of and work with.

By reading this book and considering the additional perspectives of the guest writers, you will gain a greater breadth and depth of under-standing of the world around you and hopefully take away some practical tips and resources to support your own further growth and reflection.

I hope you find this book as fun and enjoyable to read as it was to think about and write. It is meant to be thought-provoking and encourage some good conversations. If you are interested in bees I hope you are curious to learn more. If you are curious about the world of work and your role as a leader and as a role model in society, I hope this book gives you some prompts for further thinking, self-reflection and action or behaviour change.

> **Do join our book community online at**
> **www.BeeWiseBook.com**
> **to share your thoughts and connect with other readers.**

An Explanatory Note

The topics of beekeeping and leadership are vast and a great many academics and researchers spend their careers increasing the world's knowledge about both. This book brings the two topics together and the metaphor of the bees casts a new light on leadership and the new ways of working in corporate life today.

The information you will read over the coming chapters comes from many sources: a great many textbooks, first-hand experiences, and discussions with friends and fellow beekeepers. Like pollinating a wild meadow, some of these sources may be more fruitful than others and the field of research and perceived wisdom is constantly evolving! If nothing else, the more I learn the more I realise there is still a lot left to discover. This is a truism for beekeeping as well as life, particularly in the complex world of working with leaders in today's knowledge economy.

It's also important to note that throughout this book we are not anthropomorphizing bees, nor am I asking you to act more like a honey bee! They are just an interesting metaphor and an excellent opportunity for us to start thinking about our own place within a large ecosystem.

One last note: through this project, I would also like to introduce you to the work of the charity, **Bees for Development**. They help people in developing countries generate a sustainable income through beekeeping. At Hive-Logic.com Coaching & Communications we are proud to be corporate sponsors of their work. Your purchase of this book will help us to raise awareness and to continue to fund some of their campaigns. More details can be found at the end of the book.

Thank you for your interest and support!

Roof

Inner cover (crownboard)

Supers

Queen excluder

Brood box

Entrance block

Floor

Stand

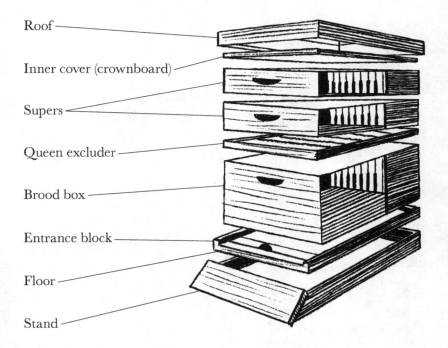

Components of a Dadant Beehive

Bee Wise

SPRING

Spring is the beginning of the annual cycle for the bees and the beekeeper. The queen will start to lay eggs as soon as the temperature begins to rise and the first telltale white blossom of the blackthorn bush appears in hedgerows in Europe. From that point the bees are in full growth phase, building combs, rearing young, foraging for nectar and pollen and starting to make honey.

Inside corporate life, the new year and spring are also the time for growth and development. Goals may be defined and budgets set.

In this section, we look at:

[1]

Organisational Design: A Working Hive

We all need to reorganise ourselves, to let go of old beliefs, processes and structures that no longer serve us.

– BILL ANDERSON, as CEO of Roche Pharmaceuticals.
Teal Around the World keynote address, 2021.

Here, we are introduced to the honey bees' hive and use it to reflect on organisational design in the workplace today.

TODAY, you may catch sight of a modern hive sitting in an orchard, under a tree or in a field. It's a series of square wooden boxes raised off the ground with a narrow landing deck at the front, with a small entrance. The bottom of these stacked boxes is called the brood box and the boxes above are called supers, where the honey is stored.

In the brood box lives the queen bee. She is about two and a half times larger than the other bees and has only one job: to lay eggs. While she sits at the top of the hierarchy, physically she lives at the bottom of the hive, in the dark, where it's coolest. Here, she will crawl over the cells to lay her eggs, followed by an entourage of bees that will look after her. Over her entire productive life – about two to five years – she will lay up to 2,000 eggs a day: more than her own body weight.

Bees naturally climb upwards, so to stop the queen from laying eggs in the boxes above, a grill with very narrow apertures is put in place, which only the smaller worker bees can climb through. You don't want the queen laying her eggs in your honey. It doesn't work, and it doesn't look good on your toast either.

The female worker bees make up the majority of the hive. Of the 30,000 to 70,000 bees found in a hive, approximately 90% of them will be female worker bees, and they will be working hard to look after the larvae and the queen in the main brood box or making honey in the supers. Each of these supers will hold eight or ten frames that have a honeycomb-patterned wax sheet suspended inside them. The frames hang vertically in the box and the worker bees will build their cells on the wax sheets. What's beautiful about these cells is that when built, they are all perfectly angled at six degrees up from the horizontal so that fresh runny honey doesn't drip out.

Then, there are the drones. Big and bulky male bees with huge bulging eyes that touch in the middle. They are called drones because that describes the deeper sounds their wings make when flying, due to their greater size. They don't do any work and can't feed themselves. They are not even able to sting. All they do is be fed honey and wait for an opportunity to mate with the queen. Once a drone has insemi-nated a queen, it dies in victory. Other drones will fly around in packs looking for other queens to mate with. At the end of the summer, when the drones are no longer necessary, they are forcibly ejected or left to starve by the female worker bees.

Every bee has its role, and every bee serves a purpose. Their organisational design is impeccable.

Most large corporations today are based on a similar hierarchy and organisational structure, with a characteristic pyramid shape. Some of those that have succeeded have been in business for over 100 years and have been celebrating centenaries. They go back to a time when early capitalist business owners, obsessed with structure, productivity and systems, looked to bees and their hives as a prime example of an ideal productive system. In 1867, Victorian satirist George Cruikshank drew a cartoon called *The British Beehive*.[1] In the drawing, fifty-four professions were divided into nine layers and organised into a hierarchy with the most important profession at the top (Queen Victoria) and

The British Bee Hive. © Trustees of the British Museum.

---

1 George Cruikshank, *The British Beehive* (London: William Tweedie, 1867).

each one below organised by perceived importance and value to Victorian society. For the Victorians at the top of the system, viewing society as a hierarchy worked and it reinforced their view of the world.

Capitalist business owners at this time assumed the most profitable working conditions were those that allowed workers to repeat the same processes again and again. To maximise profits they needed to control external variables like the supply of labour, the supply of resources, the need to generate innovation and the ability to influence government regulations. They believed you needed to monitor, observe and understand how processes could be shaped in such a way as to create maximum productivity, capturing and harvesting the value of their workers in the most efficient way.

So, to control such complexity and uncertainty, success was achieved by building order, structures and teams: a command-and-control hierarchy. For the early capitalists, this worked very well. Frederick Winslow Taylor, a Victorian industrial psychologist, observed workers and noted that there were patterns in how they completed their tasks and moved around a workspace.[2] He proposed designing factories to support this discovery and it became a great step forward in productivity. The theory was that this is how organisations would succeed.

This worked well for many business owners for over 100 years, and we saw the growth of large multinational organisations characterised by great stability and hierarchy. But it was a mechanistic approach to a productivity problem.

It assumed people in an industrial economy were no more than cogs in a machine, merely there to produce things quicker and faster. To get better results, you just needed to incentivise them with a bonus. The more experience you had, the more incentives you could have.

---

2 Frederick Winslow Taylor, *The Principles of Scientific Management*. (New York and London: Harper & Brothers, First published 1911, linked version published in 1919). https://archive.org/details/principlesofscie00taylrich.

At the top of the hierarchy was the boss: someone paid more because they were meant to know more and be the most valuable. They were the one person who could decide everything. They would have status and everything that came with it.

But in actual fact, why would the boss know what's best? You can't assume one person knows more than everybody else. And you can't assume one person – or one organisation – has all the resources, ideas and thinking to solve everything. In the current environment, I believe this model is no longer fit for purpose.

The economy has evolved in many ways since the Industrial Revolution but not in all sectors or regions of the world. This book focuses on the new growth areas of the economy: scientific research, technology, engineering, communications, robotics and digital media, for example, which is where the Hive-Logic team's work and experience are. The majority of the work we do today is focused on more complex things that require better thinking.

But we're still using outdated mindsets and principles.

Today, we work in a knowledge economy, not a mechanistic one. Success, productivity and value will come from working with the people who have the best knowledge, mindset, curiosity and creativity to solve new problems. They won't always be the people who sit at the top of the hierarchy.

For the best people to do their best work, they require psychological safety: a space to think better, where they can speak up and share their knowledge. A command-and-control model won't work if that's what's needed. The solution is a paradigm shift – in fact, two are needed: a physical shift and a mindset shift.

Physical

The old hierarchy follows a pyramid structure. It has a strong base with one person at the top: it's stable and immovable – but also inflexible. Most organisations with a pyramid-like shape have such heavy departmental structures they can't keep up with faster, more agile organisations. Just think about expenses. If I took colleagues out for dinner, my expenses would go up to my boss to be signed. And then his expenses would go up to his boss. And then a copy needs to be sent to finance and a copy to accounting … That dinner might have cost £50; why does it need to go through this process? What is the value of spending so much time controlling something so minor? Is that a good use of people's intellect and experience? Wouldn't it be great if I could be trusted by the organisation to make a decision on behalf of the organisation and do my best work?

Today, knowledge organisations must be flexible. They need to be able to move, think fast and adapt. Big organisations are now competing against start-ups, virtual organisations and even AI (Artificial Intelligence), so they need to be able to make decisions quicker, form new teams faster, and be liberated enough to respond to external stimuli with greater agility.

But to do that you need less hierarchy and less structure, and that means removing layers. We need to break the traditional pyramid structure and use a flatter one.

Mindset

In today's knowledge economy, the old command-and-control hierarchy is no longer the right mental framework to be working with either. But making this change will be a big evolutionary step because it requires us to let go of old behaviours and acknowledge that we're experiencing tension in moving from one type of working economy to the other. If controlling, measuring and approving is not the way to add value, then the question is, as an individual leader, what is your purpose? What is your value if not to command and control?

It's like a trapeze. We're flying through the air, having let go of the trapeze at one end but we haven't yet grabbed the new trapeze. In this space in the middle, there may be fear as we let go of old models and structures that gave us security. We see many leaders stuck in this space, struggling to hold on to the old and not adapting to the new. That's why at the moment, we're observing a lot of mental health problems and a high level of burnout, reactive behaviours and anxiety. In the knowledge economy, you may no longer be the subject matter expert, or at the top of the hierarchy. That can be very threatening. It's different. Absolutely terrifying. (This has also often been the case for many women in an unequal society.) But you need to find a different way of adding value, and we will talk more about that throughout this book.

In today's flatter organisational structure, your status and value will come from doing a good job and being a good co-worker. It means instead of *capturing* and *harvesting* value you need to *create* value. And that could mean being the person who initiates working with universities, opening up your intellectual property for crowdsourcing or seeking input from younger colleagues, who are closer to the customers but without the benefit of your experience. Or it could mean working with AI to bring in new ideas.

In a knowledge economy, the best ideas won't come from one person at the top of the hierarchy but from opening up and reaching outside your organisation to collaborate. It requires bringing people in who are brilliant, trusting them, and creating spaces that allow them to be brilliant. This may be seen as threatening or liberating, depending on your mental framework.

If we look to the bees, there is a theory that a hive is not 50,000 individual animals but one complex superorganism. Like the bees, we are all living organisms and when we work together in a big organisation, we create a complex superorganism – one that constantly evolves, grows and adapts to all external stimuli. When we work within an organisation that can adapt, we are far more resilient to the inevitable challenges and changes we will all experience.

Traditionally, a hierarchical command-and-control organisation served its shareholders. To give the greatest value and benefit from economies of scale, giant factories were created with employees playing the role of an interchangeable cog in a machine. To make the machines operate more efficiently, organisations worked people harder or replaced them. That was the mechanistic view.

Today, our economies are largely knowledge based, and for non-mechanistic organisations to remain fit for purpose they must adapt.

They have to evolve their structures and mental models.

To thrive, we all have to evolve.

Response

by Timm Urschinger to
Organisational Design: A Working Hive

Timm is well known as the founder of LIVEsciences and co-founder, together with Hive-Logic, of the Teal Around the World festival. The Teal Around the World Festival celebrated new ways of working and the work of Frederic Laloux's Reinventing Organizations. *He is currently a partner at EY's Enterprise Transformation Practice in Switzerland.*

Philip's metaphor of the beehive emphasises the importance of clear roles and responsibilities. In a beehive there are no lengthy meetings about what the queen bee is doing or what the drones are doing; every bee is clear on their role. This is completely unlike many organisations where discussions and decisions often take months (or longer). A queen is not supervising her workers either and she doesn't measure and track their work. Everyone is just doing their job.

This is obviously unlike the Victorian business model Philip raises in the chapter. The Victorians had another approach for their industrial economy, but that's because it was a different world, generally speaking, with very different literacy levels, education of workers, etc. The world was probably a little simpler than it is today. Now the world is far more complex and the higher the complexity gets, the less you can plan for it. And that means, for organisations, you need more adaptability.

Big organisations, from Victorian times to now, were and are built for stability, and not necessarily for adapting to whatever happens. We live at a different pace today. For example, the time it took for the telephone, after its invention, to reach fifty million users was about half a century but it only took about twelve years for the mobile phone, about eight months for TikTok and one month for ChatGPT to achieve the same numbers. There's no arguing we live at a different pace. So if that hypothesis is true, how do you plan for the next five, eight, ten, twelve years? How do you build a non-Victorian, adaptable business model?

There's one part I find interesting, which is that Philip says today you need less hierarchy and less structure in order to become more adaptable. On the one hand, yes: if everyone knows what they're supposed to be doing, why do you need several layers of hierarchy? But do we need less structure? I wouldn't necessarily agree. Without structure there is chaos. But I think you need a different kind of structure: a paradigm shift. A move from a structure of control and measurement to a structure that creates clarity, autonomy and adaptability. It's still structured but in a totally different way.

When my company and I work with clients, we help that paradigm shift by getting organisations to restructure from organising people to organising work. By organising work first, you bring clarity back to a role. Instead of asking, do I need ten people instead of twenty people, the question is, what's the work? And what's needed to get that done? And then who can do that?

When you lead an organisation that is structured to create autonomy and clarity, it means a leader's purpose is not to control and measure but to provide a vision and a direction. It means encouraging principle-based working, which means being really clear on the principles that the organisation operates by and then starting to trust people to operate based on these principles. That's how you create flexibility and autonomy.

However, having less control and less measurement can lead to more uncertainty for the individual. So that means dealing with uncertainty becomes a critical skill. If you can control, or even just have the perception of control, everything feels much better. But for an organisation to survive, adapt and become resilient its members need to develop the skill of navigating uncertainty and discomfort and that will require a high level of self-awareness and learning for everybody. It's important to emphasise this is about *navigating* uncertainty, not managing it. It's impossible to manage something you can't control.

One framework I find interesting to help with this comes from a 2011 *Harvard Business Review* article that talks about failure.[3] It presents a scale of what failure means and where it comes from. On one end of the scale, if failure comes from not paying attention, then that's not good failure. We don't want to do that in an organisational context. But then, on the other end of the scale, there's the idea of setting out to see what works. Having a hypothesis, setting up an experiment and seeing if it works. So if you then fail, it's not because of a lack of attention or skill; it's part of your organisation's evolution. You need an experimental mindset for uncertainty because logically you can't control uncertainty, but you can learn and then adjust to things that happen. By doing that you lead a more flexible organisation, where workers have more autonomy and you are creating direction, through values and principles. It is a more human-led, less mechanical and more modern approach to business.

---

3 Amy C Edmondson. *Strategies for Learning from Failure*. Harvard Business Review 89, no. 4 (April 2011).

[2]

Communication:
The Waggle Dance

*The single biggest problem in communication is
the illusion that it has taken place.*

– attributed to GEORGE BERNARD SHAW.

*In this chapter, we will reflect on how bees use the waggle dance to communicate
and apply this to our own communication style. (Bees also communicate using
pheromones but for this chapter, we're going to focus on bee communication
using movement.)*

I T WAS ARISTOTLE WHO, over two and a half thousand years
ago, first described how bees seem to communicate with each
other. However, it wasn't properly understood until 1973 when
the Austrian scientist Karl von Frisch was awarded the Nobel Prize
for his research on the honey bee waggle dance.[4] This unique form of
communication allows bees to share information precisely and efficiently
about the location of food sources with tens of thousands of nest mates.

---

4 Karl von Frisch, *Decoding the Language of the Bees.* Nobel Lecture (1973).
https://www.nobelprize.org/uploads/2018/06/frisch-lecture.pdf, accessed 02 October 2024.

When worker bees are in the role of being a scout, their job is to find a good source of pollen: say, a beautiful purple lavender in late July. When they locate a source, they will return to the hive and tell their story to the rest of the bees.

Their waggle dance indicates not only the direction and distance of the rich source of pollen, but through their energy and enthusiasm they also communicate just what a gold mine it really is. The worker bee will repeat this dance many times, and the duration of this dance is thought to indicate the quality of the flower patch. How enthusiastically she dances, and how much nectar and pollen is still stuck to her when she does this dance, will only add to the strength of her message.

The waggle dance takes the form of a figure of eight, with two round circles and a straight run in the middle. When the bee moves forward on the straight run, she waggles back and forth and this shows the approximate distance to the source of pollen. She will then turn right to circle back to the start, do another run, and then turn left and circle back creating a figure of eight. The angle of her dance in relation to that straight run will tell the bees which direction, relative to the sun, they need to fly.

If it's a gold mine, a second round of bees will go to investigate, and a third, and very quickly, thousands of bees will turn up at the same site from the same hive. On returning to the hive there are more bees to tell of the riches they have found. The message is magnified in proportion to the number of bees and the richness of the source.

The interesting thing to note is that all of this communication happens in the dark inside a noisy, busy hive, in the narrow, confined spaces between the frames of honey stores and egg cells. The bees are using their antennae, and the sounds around them, to share and receive information while all around them bees are working, buzzing, hatching, building and nursing.

Clearly, it's not an easy environment to communicate in.

Let's pause, take a step back from the buzzing and the bees, and ask: what does this mean for us as humans?

Communication is about clarity: understanding what is being asked of you and what the end result should be. However, like the bees, communication doesn't happen in isolation, and this is why it often fails.

If we think about a busy day at work, while we might not be kept in the dark or forced into six-millimetre gaps, that may be how it feels when we're caught between meetings, or when we have multiple messages, social media channels and Post-it notes to deal with. When we communicate with colleagues and peers, it's in a pressurised, busy and complex hive-like environment. The path between you and the person you're talking to (or writing to) is rarely smooth. Just as in the beehive, sometimes there are gaps in communication or obstacles in the way. After all, the biggest misconception about communication is the 'illusion that it has taken place'.

When a single scout bee comes back and tries to convince tens of thousands of nest mates to visit a new pollen site, they can tell their story as clearly as possible and can dance it as passionately as they want. But unless it's received, it's a wasted message. Therefore, communication is not just a question of message sent, it's about message *received*.

To ensure we are heard, we need to be consistent in what we say and how we say it, and we may need to repeat our own waggle dance many times. It's not enough to assume the job is finished once your message has been broadcast. It's your responsibility to ensure the message has been received and has landed appropriately. If it hasn't, it's important to listen to feedback and invite a response. We should all increase our own self-awareness of how we communicate and course correct when needed. Increasing that awareness means we will need to consider not just what we say but how we say it.

When bees communicate using the waggle dance, their level of enthusiasm and physicality expresses their level of excitement about a source of pollen. It helps other bees to get excited too. It's the same when humans communicate: our body language and tone of voice will say just as much as our words. According to Edgar Dale, the American educator, we remember only 20% of what we hear but 80% of what we personally experience.[5] And someone can experience a lot just by *how* you communicate.

Being aware of our body language and tone of voice doesn't always come naturally. I have observed leaders who, in the first part of their career, were very academic in the way they communicated. It was reinforced. A certain style of writing and speaking was their currency and that's how they succeeded. But after moving into a leadership role and working with large groups of people, it wasn't enough to lead just using the data. They needed to engage with people on many different levels, and that meant bringing their own emotions and beliefs into their work; their role was then about inspiring, motivating and creating stronger relationships.

This is not to say you should turn your back on your usual communication style, especially if you're the academic type. It's possible to go too far in the other direction.

We once had a client who was a very passionate and animated communicator. When she talked she used her hands and her whole

---

5 Edgar Dale, *Audio-Visual Methods in Teaching* (New York: Dryden Press, 1946).

face – as well as hundreds of pieces of data on a single PowerPoint slide. The energy and commitment she put into her speeches meant the audience would erupt into huge applause at the end. But if you asked a member of her audience what the presentation was about they'd say, 'I couldn't tell you'.

No one could retell her information in their own words. The sheer amount of energy she put into communicating was overwhelming her audience and they weren't able to say what her message actually was. She had the difficult but necessary challenge of needing to reduce the emotion and distil her message down to some of the clearer facts.

Being able to passionately communicate your message doesn't matter if people are unable to grasp and retell the key points of the story. When you have a message it needs to be clear and simple enough to reach everyone who needs to hear it.

Effective communication also needs to be at the right pace and intensity to be received well. If you have a presentation to do, and you are short on time, don't think rushing through the rest of the data or speaking even faster is the solution. Ask: 'In the five minutes we've got left, what else do you want to know?' Or: 'Can I just check on everyone's understanding so far?' You need to make sure that, if all else fails, your audience goes home with the most important data they need to have that day, and that they can retell it in their own words. Like the bees, we need to be able to retell and spread a consistent message.

My colleagues and I have noticed many leaders fall into a knowledge trap: they're so close to a situation or an argument they just assume everyone else knows what they know. They don't stop to check that people understand them.

Alexander was a senior medical leader who was so passionate about the results of his study that he hadn't acknowledged other people might not understand it. They needed a simplified version or a one-slide summary, not because they weren't intelligent enough to understand it, but because they needed to be able to position his message within the context of all their own work.

For Alexander, this was frustrating. The *whole topic* was important to him. He believed everybody needed *all* the data in *every single detail*. Just like he did.

But it's rare to be in a situation where everyone is interested in everything.

When you have a lot to communicate, it's best to distil your message down to the very essence: what is the *one* thing *everyone* needs to know? Tell that effectively, and then for the people who are curious or need to know more, you can offer that as an option at a separate time.

Invite curiosity in a one-to-one setting and ask open questions to understand where a person is on the spectrum of interest: how important is this to you? What does this mean for your work? What other data do you need to see? What would help you tell this story to your colleagues?

Very quickly, by using this more deliberate method, Alexander was able to spread the word far more effectively across a large, busy hive of an organisation.

The best communication is about relationships, and it involves, if possible, all the different emotions and senses that appeal to humans. That's why the best storytellers engage at an emotional level. Think of all the stories you know. It's likely you remember them because the stories evoke an *emotional* response. These memorable words have been popularly attributed to Maya Angelou: 'I've learned that people will forget what you said, people will forget what you did, but people will never forget how you made them feel.'

But sometimes, we have to communicate in the dark without emotions or our senses to help us. With the knowledge economy comes more virtual offices and an increased reliance on technology. If you're sending an email, you are broadcasting into the dark. You've no idea how it's received or when. Working on Zoom means you can see only a small part of a person's response. You can't see their foot tapping anxiously out of sight, perhaps. You can only see what's inside the frame of your screen (if they choose to be on video) and only hear them when they unmute.

Our increased use of technology has, in a way, dulled some of our senses and our ability to communicate. That's why we need to be even simpler and more compelling in how we do it. It's an art and a science, and I encourage you to spend more time thinking about how we can all convey our message most effectively.

Successful communication doesn't take place until it's triggered a helpful response in the other person. So stop, pause and think – has the message been received and understood as it was intended? If you didn't get the response you expected, do you need to adapt your communication style? Do you need to course correct? The communication style that has served you well until now might not be the right style for what is needed at this moment – or in the future, so keep learning as communicators and as leaders. If you're excited by it and it's an important message, learn from the bees: don't forget to put your energy into sharing your passion.

Response

by Jo Filshie Browning to
Communication: The Waggle Dance

Jo is one of the world's most experienced spokesperson trainers. She's a leading expert in the science of authority, and has trained top-level CEOs and thousands of professionals across the world to speak with impact and clarity. She is a TEDx speaker and author of the bestseller Scientifically Speaking: How to Speak About Your Research with Confidence and Clarity.

Communication is central to the operation of any organisation or community. That's why I loved that Philip included the idea of the waggle dance and the critically important role it plays for the hive. The waggle dance is a form of communication and if it isn't precise and clear, the bees won't be able to find the pollen – which means the hive won't survive.

The stakes are high for a hive. But they're also high for an organisation because in order to succeed, you need everyone pulling in the same direction towards the same goal. And to make that happen, you need clarity of communication. Leaders must be clear and thoughtful about how they communicate so their teams understand what's expected of them.

So for me, the critical question for a leader is always, 'What is my goal?' and specifically, 'What do I want my audience to do?'

When we're communicating, we're essentially asking people to change. We're asking people to do something, and that's why we need to think very specifically about what they need to hear to be motivated to do that. Rather than being told to just do it, how do we get them to *want* to do it? How do we inspire them?

Research shows people generally don't make decisions based on facts alone. The majority of our decisions actually have an emotional component. This means that to be compelling, our messaging must speak not just to people's minds but also to their hearts. So how do we communicate in a way that generates emotion?

One method you can use to begin your plan for impactful communication is a simple three-step process called Think, Feel, Do.

Before you communicate, identify specifically who you're speaking with. Then ask:

- What do I want them to *think?*
- What do I want them to *feel?*
- What do I want them to *do?*

Answering these questions will help you to begin to understand what you need to say in order to start moving people towards your goal. For example, if you want people to feel excited about something, you might choose to use vocabulary which is positive and forward-facing.

Lack of communication skills is a real limiting factor for leaders, no matter how well-meaning or impactful they could potentially be. If you have a ten-out-of-ten idea but your communication skills are a four out of ten, there's no way you will ever communicate your ten-out-of-ten idea adequately. If people don't understand or connect with your idea, then they won't be inspired to take your idea on board and act accordingly.

When you look at great leaders, universally you'll find they're also great communicators. There's no right or wrong way to create impact, so they may have different styles but they're all able to create clarity, enthusiasm and, most importantly, emotion.

Your end goal as a leader is shaped by the impact you have on people. It's the reason you're communicating in the first place, but your impact depends on whether people go away thinking, feeling and doing exactly what you need them to. The reality is that after you've finished speaking, something will happen, whether you like it or not. Your audience might do exactly what you want – or they might ignore you or question you. If your communication isn't precise, you haven't just created confusion: you've also wasted time as people come back to ask, 'Can I just check what you meant by that?'

The cost of time wasted to clarify a communication afterwards can be enormous, so it's incredibly important to invest in getting it right for your audience. Having a clear road map for where you want people to go is the first step towards sending them off on the right journey. When you think things through in advance and take time to fully understand your audience and plan the road ahead, it pays dividends in saved time, effort, money and morale.

Leaders who are accomplished communicators can make it seem natural and effortless. But what people might not know is that many leaders work with people like Philip and me for hours, or even days, to ensure their critical communications are clear and impactful. Of course, the final communication looks effortless, but it's a bit like Fred Astaire's extraordinary dancing. In his words: 'I suppose I made it look easy, but gee whiz, did I work and worry!'

So to sum up, what I'd like to add to this chapter is to emphasise the importance of strategy and practice when it comes to spoken communication. Preparation is critical. And the secret is that most of the leaders we see, who are excellent communicators, are that way because they prioritise preparation and make time for it. Understandably, that's not something they would ever advertise. You're unlikely to hear a senior leader quietly admit they spent the whole morning with their communications coach. But in reality, there are hours spent supporting people to prepare and be at their best for the most important on-the-record moments. Mark Twain said it perfectly when he noted: 'It usually takes me more than three weeks to prepare a good impromptu speech.'

I often think of communication as the electricity that runs through a system. You seldom notice it but if it's not there, or if it's not working well, then everything stops. Or you can think of it like mortar that holds the bricks together so the organisation can stand. Without it, when there's pressure, everything can collapse. As a leader, communication is not only an area that's central to your success – it's an area that's under your full control. If you want to connect with your audience, create clarity and make an impact, then time spent prioritising and preparing your communications is time well spent.

[3]

Creativity:
Pollination

Learning and innovation go hand in hand.
The arrogance of success is to think that what you
did yesterday will be sufficient for tomorrow.

– WILLIAM POLLARD, 1932.

We're all aware of the importance of pollination for our environment, and in
this chapter we use it as a metaphor for pollination of ideas and creativity. We
will think about the importance of drawing from different sources of inspiration
and how that can build a stronger organisation.

E'RE ALL FAMILIAR WITH the buzz of bees on a beautiful
spring day. When we see an orchard full of apple trees
with white blossoms, or weeks later, the cherry blossoms
in their lovely pink petals, we can hear the buzzing of bees, and it seems
like the whole tree is alive.

This is because most bees in a hive will go to a single source of pollen.

When scout bees find a good source and tell their hive, an entire tree can be pollinated very quickly by the same colony of bees.

But let's pause and think for a moment about what the bees are doing. It would be inefficient for a bee to fly randomly to each tree and go into every single flower to see which ones have been pollinated and which ones haven't. So how do they know which flower to aim for?

Using static electricity, the smell of pollen, ultraviolet light and information from other bees, these little creatures can very quickly decide which flower to visit.

The static charge also helps bees to gather pollen more efficiently. The mechanism of pollen transfer differs by species of bee and flowers, but essentially when a bee flies through the air it creates a positively charged electrical field. Flowers, and pollen, are negatively charged and as the bee nears the flower, the force of attraction causes the pollen to jump from flower to bee. Often a whole bee's body will become completely covered in pollen that sticks to its hairy thorax as it visits multiple flowers on a single tree. For plants that are very rich sources of pollen, the bees land in the flower and collect the brightly coloured grains in the pollen sacs on their hind legs, ready to transport in large quantities back to the hive. The bees then visit many different flowers and plants of the same species; for example, neighbouring cherry trees in an orchard. This is advantageous for many flower and plant species as the act of cross-pollination produces more genetic diversity, and therefore resilience and sustainability for the plants.

This in itself is an interesting metaphor: innovation can rarely be optimally developed by an individual. In Steven Johnson's great book, *Where Good Ideas Come From*, he explores the natural history of innovation and how new ideas can emerge and be harnessed for success.[6] He suggests that good ideas do not – for the most part – come from inside one person's head. Instead, they come from outside, specifically from social interaction. As coaches, we strongly encourage all senior leaders we work with to have more people they can have discussions with. It could be a formal coaching relationship, it could be a mentor, it could be a sponsor. A friend, peer or family member would also work. The important thing is to 'socialise' an idea and gain new perspectives and feedback.

Everyone can benefit from actively seeking out mentors and sponsors who can help bring fresh ideas to your organisation, but also to how you view your role. The work we do is often about coaching, and that's a very specific skill, whereas mentoring and sponsorship are different. We've noticed lots of organisations have mentors or mentoring systems, but the relationship is rarely well defined. The mentor doesn't really understand their mentoring role, and the mentee often doesn't know what they're asking for.

Coaching and mentoring are development methods to support you to reflect, identify and achieve your goals. Both are valuable in enabling you to improve working relationships, enhance your performance, develop your capability and manage your career. Coaching or mentoring partnerships aim to complement rather than replace the support of a line manager.

---

6 Steven Johnson, *Where Good Ideas Come From: The Seven Patterns of Innovation* (London: Penguin Books, 2011).

Coaching

The International Coaching Federation (ICF, coachingfederation.org) defines coaching as 'partnering with clients in a thought-provoking and creative process that inspires them to maximize their personal and professional potential'. The process of coaching assumes a client is fundamentally resourceful and is able to access sources of imagination, productivity and leadership to help themselves develop. In a pure coaching relationship the coach does not provide answers or experience but the framework and space for a client to own their own success.

Mentoring

The Chartered Institute of Personal Development (CIPD, cipd.org) defines mentoring as 'a relationship in which a more experienced colleague uses their greater knowledge and understanding of the work or work environment to support the development of a more junior or inexperienced member of staff'. The mentor may share their own experience or practical support, such as introductions and contacts.

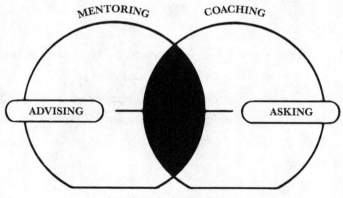

Mentoring vs. Coaching Venn Diagram

We strongly encourage mentors and mentees to explicitly discuss and agree what it is they expect of each other when they first meet. A mentor-mentee relationship isn't just about having lunch every few months; it's about the mentor knowing exactly what it is they need to offer, and the mentee knowing what they need to ask for. The mentor and mentee would do well to have a 'contracting' discussion about how they can both contribute and get the best out of the valuable relationship.

Reverse mentoring can be very valuable too. Mentoring is often assumed to involve an older, more senior person mentoring a younger, more junior person. It's easy to assume the people with the most value to offer are the ones more senior than us or older than us, and that's because we've been brought up in an old-fashioned model where we turn to our parents or senior bosses, who are older than us, for guidance.

But that's not always the case. We can all benefit from the perspective of a different generation, with a different work-life model. With the increasing pace of technological change, maybe our role models should be people who are younger than us and who are adapting to life in a different way to how older leaders are. After all, we are in a knowledge economy and it's reasonable to assume someone younger than us will have expertise in an area we do not.

Separate to a mentor is the notion of having someone who's a sponsor: having someone in an organisation who is looking out for you from a career perspective. Who can support you and use their status or leadership to help advance your opportunities? That's a different relationship. But still a two-way relationship. Fundamentally, I don't agree with the distinction that age equals 'better' (unless we're talking about cheese), but the principle is important: everyone should seek to open their hearts and their eyes and their ears and all of their senses to other people's experiences.

Putting all your energy into doing a good job doesn't mean you should lose yourself in a single task. In Alsace during April, we get huge mono-culture fields filled with these amazing bright yellow flowers. It looks beautiful on one of those early, hot spring days and the bees go crazy for it. It's intoxicating.

But in actual fact, it's not very good for the bees.

These yellow fields are filled with rapeseed (known as colza in French, or canola in the United States) – one of the first big flowering crops. While it may look wonderful on a spring day, unfortunately, it doesn't make very good honey. It forms a very short chain sugar that sticks solid, and it can clog up the whole of a hive. It tastes absolutely awful and is difficult to extract. Rapeseed is also subject to very high use of pesticides, which may affect a bee's neuroprocessing causing them to become disorientated. Sadly, this confusion means they are unlikely to return to the hive safely and will likely die. As a beekeeper, the best thing to do is to take the honey out and throw it away. Relying on a single source of pollen is not good for anyone.

Bees, and the honey they make, flourish best in a beautiful open meadow of wildflowers, where there's great ecological diversity. In cities, a combination of natural cherry trees, lime trees or linden trees, plus window boxes, can also fuel diversity and the bees. Every great idea is a cross-pollination or a mutation of an idea that has already been brought to life.

These are the building blocks of innovation and great ideas, not individual thoughts. So, go to a coffee shop and talk with a friend who works in a different industry. Ask a fresh pair of eyes for an opinion, or investigate things that have surprised you. Ideas improve and come to life when they are adopted, understood and improved by other people and these can all lead to even more new ideas.

What new technologies or possibilities have emerged in the last year that you haven't considered?

What path have you not taken?

What unusual, unpredictable, disconnected idea could you try next?

A bit like the bees, you are relying on the input of other people to share ideas and information about what the next steps should be. This might be stretching the metaphor, but the apple trees are only in blossom for a couple of weeks and then it's gone for that year. Where will the next source of pollen come from? What else have you got? Once the scout bees have found a good source, they're already on to the next source of pollen. So, it's important to ask yourself: what else do I need to consider? Who do I need to speak to? What do I need to do next?

That may mean taking a different approach to the task at hand, whether self-development and learning or a project you're currently engaged in. We all have a responsibility as individuals to look out and scan the horizon and see what is coming. But if we can work as a collective regardless of rank or role, we will have a much smoother and more efficient working team.

Change your environment and change your inputs. Ideas and innovation don't always come from looking forward or back; rather, they come from looking left and right, to what is adjacent to us. I know of meetings where a chance miscommunication has led to a flourishing of new ideas and fresh approaches. A misunderstanding can sometimes yield the best results; don't leave any stone unturned.

Johnson builds on Stuart Kauffman's[7] concept of the 'adjacent possible' to reaffirm that tomorrow's great innovations will be built from the stuff of today – the things around us that can be combined into something new. So, whether you're at an organisational level or a personal level, throw yourself in. Get covered in pollen. Be as excited, engaged and enthusiastic as those hard-working bees. You never know what fruitful ideas you might have.

---

7 Stuart A. Kauffman, *Investigations* (Oxford: Oxford University Press, 2000).

Response

by Ricardo Troiano to Creativity: Pollination

Ricardo is the co-founder of leadership advisory firm Concio.com, which works to support leaders and multinational organisations through change and transformation. He has lived on three continents and in four countries, starting as an engineer, then moving on to management consulting in learning, leadership, strategy and change practice, followed by a leading global industry role focused on change and organisational development.

As Philip writes above: 'The act of cross-pollination between different plants produces more genetic diversity, and therefore resilience and sustainability for the plants.' Remove 'genetic' and substitute 'plants' with 'organisation' and this is the very spirit of this chapter, and the very focus of much of our collective work with leaders. It's these simple, yet often illusive, concepts that are at the heart of maintaining a thriving organisation – and apparently, a healthy beehive as well!

In the last few days, as I sit to write this, I've been travelling through France's Provence region, just as the lavender fields are hitting the peak of their beauty. One thing that stands out as I walk among the purple and violet-hued fields is the ever-present buzzing of bees. They're everywhere and their sounds have a visceral quality, resonating well beyond my ears. As I taste the local lavender-flavoured gelato and sample local honey, I feel incredibly grateful for all of their hard work.

But as we read, one cannot live on lavender alone! It is diversity that expands the joy in life, maintains a healthy beehive and similarly, brings innovative thinking into organisations.

The key is whether organisations can tap into that, and both nurture and develop it across an entire value chain and over the long term. Enter inclusion and equity. This is the real work that makes diversity deliver on the promise of adding tangible and sustained business value. Like bees turning pollen into fuel for their hive, organisations must tap into the breadth of their diverse workforce to capitalise on the innovation that will fuel sustained growth.

When it comes to resilience and sustainability, I'd offer that they are two sides of the same coin. Every system will undoubtedly meet with difficulties as it strives to survive and thrive. The ability to meet, engage with and overcome these challenges will define the long-term health of the system.

While organisations often spend time and energy attempting to predict and plan for future disruptions, it is unlikely they can cover every single contingency. I'd assume this is similar to a beehive that can't accurately predict the weather, or understand what other threats may be lurking around the corner. Ultimately, it won't be the most accurate predictors that survive but those that are most adaptable and resilient. The ones that can bounce back quickly from adversity and learn from it.

We often confuse a learning organisation with organisational learning. The former is about fostering an environment for growth through prioritisation of ongoing learning, while the latter is about learning from both success and failure in a way that fosters the very resilience that drives sustainable growth. I've seen too many organisations fail to embed this learning and get stuck in the loop of continuously tinkering with strategy, operating models and leadership shifts, only to repeat previous errors. As Nietzsche once wrote: 'Our treasure lies in the beehive of our knowledge.'[8] For sure, good knowledge management is worth its weight in honey!

Finally, we get to innovation: the fuel that ties these concepts together. Bringing in the 'new' that will ensure progress always finds a way. Much like the bees thriving from a variety of flora to pick from, broadening the channels for innovation is what may ultimately have the biggest positive impact.

I'm reminded of the stories, picked from the central thesis of David Epstein's book, *Range*, that showcase how people who think broadly and embrace diverse experiences and perspectives will increasingly thrive.[9] The examples we are all undoubtedly familiar with include Leonardo da Vinci, threading his genius across art, engineering, architecture and science. Or perhaps Marie Curie, pulling her innovative thinking from a blend of her deep understanding of physics, chemistry and mathematics. More recently, we saw the same thing with Steve Jobs, whose insights that drove tremendous market value came out of weaving together his expertise in technology, design and marketing. Each had a diverse set of varied skills and experiences that, when combined, made the outcome spectacular and memorable.

As for myself, I feel I've fuelled my own learning similarly through a diverse set of life and career paths. Having lived on three continents and in four countries, I've pulled from a variety of cultures, including the learnings from my Glaswegian mother and my Argentine father. As for my career, I started as an engineer in power transmission, then spent a couple of decades in Big Four management consulting focusing

---

8 Friedrich Nietzsche, *On the Genealogy of Morals*, trans. Douglas Smith (Oxford: Oxford University Press, 1998 [1887]), 3.

9 David Epstein, *Range: How Generalists Triumph in a Specialized World* (London: Macmillan, 2019).

on learning, leadership, strategy and change practice, followed by an industry role focused on change and organisational development, and most recently, I set off as an entrepreneur, launching a leadership advisory company with a partner. Beyond that, I owe my growth to an unquenchable curiosity about all things and how they work. I expect the key for me will be to keep bumping around into others who think and find their interests in different areas, in the hope that I will continue the learning journey.

SUMMER

Summer is a time when the hive is working at full capacity. Wild meadows hum to the sound of busy bees. Trees such as lime and acacia are in full bloom. A colony of bees may peak at over 30,000 individual members, all working as one macroorganism. A new queen may be reared, and a colony may also reproduce by forming a swarm.

Inside organisations we may be halfway through an annual plan, new products may be launched, and key milestones should have been met. It's also a time for summer vacation and reflection.

In this section, we look at:

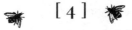

[4]

Productivity:
Busy as a Bee

How doth the little busy bee, Improve each shining hour,
And gather honey all the day, From every opening flower.
... In works of Labour or of Skill, I would be busy too:
For Satan finds some Mischief still, For idle hands to do.
— ISAAC WATTS, *Against Idleness and Mischief,* 1715.

Bees are revered for their hard work and 'busy as a bee' is a common theme
throughout culture and society worldwide. In this chapter, we will review and
reflect on this idea, and think about the lessons we can learn from these bees.

TO SOME, bees are amazing, inspiring and beautiful. To others, perhaps scary. But they are always synonymous with being busy because that is all we see: bees working tirelessly from dawn to dusk, going from flower to flower.

The majority of the hive are hard-working female workers bees, and they work tirelessly, keeping the whole hive going, for the duration of their short lifetime. To create a single 500 gram jar of honey, honey bees will have collectively visited approximately 2,000,000 flowers. They will have flown 88,000 kilometres and visited up to 100 flowers in a single day. A strong bee colony can fly the equivalent distance from the Earth to the Moon every day.

Bees live their lives at a fast pace, and in the summer that's only about thirty-four days.

Then ... they go out like a bright light.

Bees are well known as symbols of energy and hard work. During the Industrial Revolution, the people of Manchester, UK, chose the bee as a symbol of their industriousness and if you ever visit, you'll find lovely little bee icons dotted around the city. In Mormon iconography, beehives are models of a hard-working society and in the United States, Utah is nicknamed the Beehive State. Its motto is 'Industry', and a beehive appears on the flag. But this isn't always a good metaphor for human endeavour.

I noticed that with clients and myself, a simple enquiry into how someone is inevitably leads to an answer: 'I'm good, thanks. I'm busy.'

Busy has become a badge of honour. A status of value. We have succumbed to the notion that being busy as a bee is how we get results, drive success and feel accomplished. We are recognised, needed and important.

But the risk with idolising the idea of being 'a busy bee' is that it becomes superficial.

When we measure our workplace value by the quantity of work we have done in a day, it's a fine line between success and overwhelm. If success only comes when you double down or speed up, that very quickly increases the risk of a mental health breakdown.

This doesn't help when we work largely within a culture that reinforces the value of quantity over quality. But if you want to increase quantity within a finite week, you need to increase speed, and we have all experienced the cultural trope in organisations (and outside of work) about the speed of doing things quickly.

While improvements in technology have helped us to reply quicker and work faster, it hasn't helped people reply *better*. The drive for speed and productivity means creating a culture of jumping into a problem before we're ready. It doesn't matter if we've not really had the time or space to think about the best way to solve it. As long as we are seen to be working efficiently.

But speed is not a bad thing. Productivity is not something we need to drop. Let's acknowledge that it's enjoyable to be productive and to get things done quickly. We get a dopamine hit from ticking things off a list. The danger comes when it becomes a habit to act before we think: to respond to emails quickly, commit to another meeting, another event, or another project without considering the long-term consequences.

When we add *more* to our list, it means we have to be *more* productive. So, we get up earlier, work faster, see less of our families, take more business trips, eat badly, forget to exercise – no wonder we're exhausted by the end of the week. The genuine enthusiasm, passion and joy that you once had for the role is quickly replaced by weariness and overwhelm. You feel torn, filled with a dispiriting feeling as the list of tasks you have to do keeps growing. Without time for rest and relaxation we are physically and mentally exhausted, which can lead to ill health and bad decision-making.

While being busy may give you a feeling of being productive, what is the value of that 'busyness'? And is that what we should aspire to?

So often when we are stuck on a hamster wheel that just goes faster and faster and faster, we are more likely to choose the quickest, easiest solution.

But not always the right solution.

As leaders, our job is to facilitate the best solution and innovative thinking, but that means we need time and space for our own creative thinking and problem-solving. That is less likely to happen if we don't have time for quietness and reflection. And this is when bad decisions are made.

Of course, work needs doing and we need to be productive and deliver on our promises, but when we rush around, we are not able to be fully present or enjoy the simple things in life like a treat of hot honey on toast, or an insightful conversation with a colleague.

When we are too busy, we miss opportunities for human connection and our relationships at work and home can become strained when we are not fully present. While we may find comfort in feeling busy, it's important to recognise all of that is just an illusion.

Your list of things to do is *just* a list of things to do.

It's your busy mind that creates your busy experience. It's your emotional and mental response to that list, and how you are triggered by the stimuli, that turns it into a frenzy of overwhelm and stressful activity.

A missed deadline often leads us to believe we have somehow disappointed people or let them down. Unread emails are *just* unread emails, but we may associate feelings of negativity with tasks unfulfilled. This then spirals into an unhealthy negative relationship with productivity and the relationship with how we provide value. We may start questioning our abilities, dramatically concluding that this is the wrong job for us.

The list of potential thoughts and feelings is enormous.

But it's essential to remember it's just noise contained inside our own framework of values, judgements and thinking, and often made worse by a work culture that reinforces and perpetuates busyness by recognising and rewarding it.

What if we can create a culture that gives us space to pause and to think a little bit better? Could we make a better-quality contribution? Would our work have a bigger impact?

We all have an individual accountability to ask: 'Are we doing the right thing here? What is the most effective way to solve this problem? Is the deadline really Friday? And if the deadline is Friday, what can we pause to meet that deadline?'

When we slow down, a problem can be better served and better solved.

I believe that pressing pause and stopping this quest for busyness will be the solution to creating a real competitive advantage and what will change our customers' lives. We need to replace our culture of 'busy-ness' with more meaningful contributions to the working world, and I acknowledge that will be hard. But sometimes we need to do the big difficult things to create change.

It's not sustainable to believe that the busier you are, the more valued you are.

We need a mindset shift that requires letting go of the old framework of 'I am valued for my busyness', and instead creating a new framework: 'The more I look after myself, and the more I look after my team, the more likely people will be in a better state to do better work.'

Your competitive advantage will not come from being busier – from being as busy as a bee – but from better thinking.

That is your competitive advantage.

It's not doing more work. It's about engaging in better thinking about bigger and more important problems.

But it's like the trapeze we talked about in Chapter 1, where we are still suspended somewhere between the two frameworks.

To reach the new framework, two things need to happen. Firstly, as an individual, you need to be confident in your ability to stop, pause and add more value. It requires authenticity, vulnerability and trust from you and the people around you, and that will also be hard. But that doesn't mean it shouldn't be done.

Secondly, from an organisational perspective, stopping and pausing needs to be allowed. If a senior leader spends time with new recruits or spends time mentoring people, that's valuable to an organisation and they will see the rewards over the long term. That needs to be celebrated. A culture of better thinking is one where people feel able to speak up, be vulnerable, and are acknowledged and recognised for it.

Let's stop using outdated metrics that measure people based on the quantity of outputs, and start measuring quality. Without this, we will never have change.

To quote Nancy Kline from *Time to Think*, 'The quality of everything we do depends on the quality of the thinking we do first.'[10] All our clients are hugely clever individuals with a lot of experience. They know all the answers, but they rarely have the time in their busy days to think about and expand on those solutions.

Who has ever had their best ideas in a meeting or in front of a laptop? I find my best ideas come to me when I'm in the shower, or cycling or

---

10 Nancy Kline, *Time to Think: Listening to Ignite the Human Mind* (London: Cassell Illustrated, 2021).

preparing vegetables. For others, it's when they have time to talk freely with a colleague, after a long walk, or with a coffee outside the office.

This shift will take time, but finding ways to acknowledge and appreciate quality outcomes rather than quantity outputs is what's needed today, especially in the knowledge economy. The alternative is spending more time doing more emails or kicking a problem from one place to another, and that adds no value.

Instead of being busy, wouldn't it be lovely if you asked how a colleague was and they said: 'I'm great, thanks. I spent the whole morning thinking about how we can make things better.' Or: 'I've had a brilliant morning, talking to new team members and understanding where they're coming from.'

This is the genesis of better-quality work.

Let's not strive to be as busy as the bees.

Response

by Martin Daubney to
Productivity: Busy as a Bee

Martin is a psychological coach based in Basel, Switzerland and author of Clear Your Head to Get Ahead. *Through his company, Inspire Coaching GmbH, he has worked with senior leaders and executives in global organisations to help them manage their stress, improving not only their performance (and mental well-being) but also the performance of their teams.*

My recommendation, at this point, is to put your copy of this book down and reflect. Slow down and think back over your working life to the times when you were being that busy bee. If you are anything like me, you will have experienced a work life with ups and downs where the demands on your time have been fully manageable, to times when you were pushed to the brink, or maybe even over the brink. And if you're like me, the chances are you soldiered on because it was expected of you.

The paradox, though, is that as we do more, become more busy and slowly drift into overwhelm, we cannot possibly show up in our best state. We don't deliver our best work and mistakes happen. Before long, we are in a downward spiral as, unlike bees, we ruminate on our day and find it difficult to experience rejuvenating sleep, only to start the next day of 'busyness' in a worse state than we left it.

If you have not experienced this pattern you will undoubtedly see it play out in others, and it happens as we're experiencing the stress response. Yes, we are stressed. The bigger problem here is that stress is contagious and by bringing in the energy of stress to the colony – or your team – you start to affect others, energetically stressing them too.

Stress shows up in my clients all the time, but they rarely know it. Most of the time we are not the first to know; the people around us are, typically our partners and work colleagues. Stress is a behavioural outlet of the emotional state: often a consequence of the environment we are in at the time. When we're experiencing too much stress we behave differently, maybe by snapping at the kids or getting on less well with colleagues. Sleep is a good clue, even if we do brush off a bad night's sleep as being just that. If the situation goes on for too long then we might also notice our digestive system is behaving in a weird or unusual way and that we're catching colds too frequently – or worse.

However, stress is also a good thing as it does help us get stuff done. It's there for our survival especially, getting us out of the burning building by suddenly running faster than we thought we ever could. It's the insidious build-up of chronic stress in the workplace that leads to exhaustion and ultimately burnout.

Pressing pause is the way to break this cycle, and it starts with you.

Before I share how to do this, you first need to accept that by doing less you will get more done. By slowing down you will meet your deadlines faster, and by shifting into a better state you will shorten meetings that generate great decisions, in less time. On a personal level, it will also reduce your blood pressure and bring in a sense of calm. I know because I have experienced all of the above. The secret lies in the fact that, unlike all the other creatures on this planet, we have the unique ability to choose how we feel. Bees clearly 'know' a lot of stuff, but they cannot choose to feel anything; they don't worry about the weather, the commute to the pollen or their productivity quotas. They just get on, do and then die, all in thirty-four days.

The way you can start to break your busyness and reclaim your life is by upping your self-awareness and developing your self-knowing. The emotional state you are in is the key to making this transformation and yet, most of us don't know what emotional state we're in at any one time. Especially men! So start by checking in with yourself and feeling your emotions. Maybe a good time to do this is after an event that either went well or not. How do you feel about the event as you reflect on it? When heading out to a meeting, an important one, ask yourself what you are feeling and if that emotional state will help you with your intended outcome. A feeling of nervousness, anxiety or fear is not the best state to be in, to be at your best.

Once you grasp the concept of self-awareness you can start to control your emotional state. Emotions are, after all, just information. They are generated to tell us something, so listen. Some emotions, you'll notice, can help us feel good, rejuvenating and increasing our energy, while others will deplete us and wear us down. So, try the following exercise.

First of all, breathe. Breathe low and slow: that is to say, a little deeper into your belly and a little slower than you might usually breathe, at a rate that is comfortable for you. Belly breathing isn't sexy, but it is good for you!

Close your eyes and focus your attention on your heart, or chest area, and imagine that breath is flowing in and out of your heart. Just so you know, this part about bringing your attention to your heart or chest area is a step to get you out of your head, to clear your mind, to stop that busy brain from being busy.

After about three breaths I invite you to step into a regenerative emotional state – one that supports you and energises you, like gratitude or appreciation for someone or something in your life – and generate all the feelings of gratitude or appreciation.

Keep this going for a few minutes, about five if you can, and open your eyes.

How did it go? How do you feel now?

The chances are you're a bit calmer, and yet still alert, than you were a few minutes ago. This would be a great state for making a decision or having a conversation with a co-worker or partner. You will be much more present, even if for just a few minutes.

The cardio and neuroscience behind this technique have been studied for about forty years now and so we know it's not only possible to shift your emotional state to be at your best every day, without burning out, but that practising this technique for just five minutes at a time, at least three times a day, will shift your system into a state known as coherence: alignment of flow. It's in this state that we slow down to achieve more: meet our goals and targets without overwhelm, make great decisions, and have a much better quantity and quality of sleep.

So please don't wait for the organisation you work for to implement this practice and don't wait for permission. Be the trailblazer. In the same way that your stressed colleague will raise the stress level in the team, you can alter the emotional thermostat in the room to your advantage and bring out your best and the best in others.

[5]

Continuous Learning:
A Worker Bee's Career

We are very largely devoted to doing the wrong thing right.
That's very unfortunate, because the righter you do the wrong thing,
the wronger you become.

– RUSS ACKOFF, 1919–2009.

In this chapter, we will reflect on a bee's working life. We will think about the
importance of learning and how it relates to our lives inside and outside of work.

AFTER A FEMALE WORKER bee hatches and leaves its egg, what comes next is a multifaceted and busy 'career' directed by hormonal changes as well as the needs of the hive. In the winter this career will span several months, but during the summer all that hard work will be compressed into a lifespan of just a single short month, on average thirty-four days.

First, as soon as they hatch, they specialise in becoming a housekeeper bee. They are trained by slightly older adult bees to look after all the cells, making sure they are clean and keeping the larvae and the brood warm. They exclusively perform that role for the first few days of their life. They then take time to train the previous set of bees that have just hatched to do the same.

Then they spend the next three to five days doing a completely different role, acting as a nanny to feed the older larvae with pollen and honey. Pollen is a protein which is also stored in the hive. The honey reserves are sugar: the carbohydrate that feeds the larvae and helps them to grow. They specialise and focus on this second task before 'retraining again' to become an expert in a different specialty, a nurse.

The nursing role is to look after and feed the young worker bees. They then, again, completely change their speciality and spend time training and teaching the previous set of bees who are just younger than them.

Next, the worker bees are trained in a completely different task, which is to be a builder. When they are builders, they use their wax glands to build the perfect hexagonal six-sided cells, angled very specifically at six degrees to the horizontal, so the immature new honey doesn't drip out. Again, another very specific task.

At this point, the worker bees have still only existed in the darkness, deep inside the hive. Gradually, in these roles, they progress to the outside of the hive and after being the builder, the next role is to be a security guard. They take a role at the front of the hive for the first time and welcome the new bees coming back from their foraging. They also prevent other animals and insects from coming into the hive. If you've ever been stung by a bee near a hive, it'll probably be a security guard that has given up its life to protect the hive. As they die in the process of stinging you, they will also emit a 'panic pheromone' so other guard bees are alerted to join the battle against a perceived foe. So, if you get stung once – watch out!

When the guard bees are standing sentry at the front of the hive, they also perform a very specific secondary role: temperature controllers. On the hottest of days, to maintain the humidity and temperature inside the hive, their role is to control ventilation. They plant their six legs firmly on the entrance to the hive and beat their wings, sucking cooler air in and drawing warm, moist air out of the hive, thereby setting up a ventilation circuit. It's an incredible sight – and noise – to see them beating their wings at full power, working at their maximum limit with their tails pointing down towards the landing board, but not actually flying. It's important to recognise that this is a very specific skill, different to being a builder, a nurse or a housekeeper.

Their final role is to be a forager. By this point, they are stationed out at the entrance to the hive and receiving data from the waggle dance performed by the incoming victorious scout bees (which we discussed in Chapter 2). When we marvel at a bee pollinating a beautiful cherry tree or balcony flowers, what you are seeing is a bee at the end of its lifespan, foraging and pollinating for the last two to three days of its life. Be kind to them. It is the end of their life's work.

Throughout the life of a bee, all individuals perform all the main functions within a hive. In case there is a crisis – maybe a hive is damaged, and the honey cells need rebuilding – the worker bees can be reallocated to specific roles at short notice to serve the needs of the colony. It isn't fully understood how this happens, but it is a focus of current research. There's an interesting parallel here for us to consider.

Life is constantly changing and so will our careers, so to avoid getting lost and overwhelmed by all these changes, we need to stop and look at the world through two different lenses: a short-term lens and a long-term lens.

The short-term lens requires us to focus on what we are doing right now and to make sure we're good at it. Therefore, we need to put energy into effective learning and changing our behaviour in a sustainable way. Swedish psychologist K. Anders Ericsson, considered to be the 'expert on experts', showed there is little evidence that superior performance can be explained by giftedness or inherent talent.[11] It is those who spend time challenging themselves, or trying things just past their level of expertise and comfort, who tend to become experts in their chosen field.

Ericsson's formula for developing expertise has five elements we can all try. First, learn and experience the task (or lesson). Then, reflect on what needs improving. Third, create objectives for development, and fourth, engage in deliberate practice for reaching those objectives. Finally, reflect on this practice to get feedback from yourself and others to find further points to develop. Repeat steps three to five as needed.

This exercise can be used as a vehicle to practice learning and to ensure we are progressing. If you've recently been given a new role, give yourself time to settle into the position and try these steps to discover what is required of you, where your strengths lie in this role and where you could improve.

Career growth doesn't come from being comfortable in a role. Tom Senninger, a German educator, suggested the recommended optimal state in which to learn can be described as being between comfort and panic.[12] This is the zone where learning occurs. So seek new challenges, try something new – that's where the most learning happens.

The long-term lens asks us to keep an eye on the horizon and be aware of what's changing in our external environment. A lot of people we work

11 K. Anders Ericsson, Neil Charness, Paul J Feltovich and Robert R. Hoffman, eds, *Cambridge Handbook of Expertise and Expert Performance* (New York: Cambridge University Press, 2006).

12 Tom Senninger developed the concept of the learning zone based on Lev Vygotsky's model of Proximal Development.

with need to be more aware of the system beyond their current role and organisation because if you've been inside one organisation for a long time, the risk is that it shapes your expectations, hopes and fears. If ever you have to leave, you may find yourself lost.

Everyone will experience this at some point in their career, especially during organisational transformations, transitions or headcount reductions. So, it's important to establish your set of values and goals based on who you are, not on the ones provided by your workplace.

As part of your career evolution, ask yourself what it is you're interested in. Where do your passions lie? Notice what you like doing and what you don't. Does your work give you joy? (Chapter 12 may help you dive deeper into this exploration.)

Through your self-reflection, if you realise you're no longer interested or curious about your role, you're probably in the wrong place; it's time to consciously make a move and get out.

I'm working with a senior leader at the moment who is a brilliant academic scientific researcher. They have loved that part of their job for two decades but as they become more senior, their role is becoming more about leadership than academic study. And they are at a junction: do they want to go deeper down the academic path? Or do they want to broaden their skills and become a leader of other scientific researchers?

It's a good dilemma to have. Just like the bees supporting the next wave of younger bees to become brilliant subject matter experts, it takes time to train others. Do you want to be the person to develop, coach, mentor and support? If so, that's a specific skill that needs to be learned and practised. However, if your superpowers truly lie in technical and academic expertise, is that where you want the rest of your career to play out?

There are two dimensions to learning and development. It is no longer a vertical process but a horizontal process too: it's T-shaped.[13]

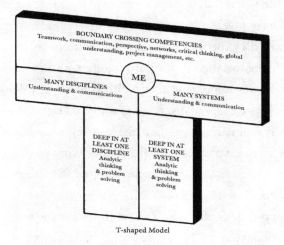

BOUNDARY CROSSING COMPETENCIES
Teamwork, communication, perspective, networks, critical thinking, global understanding, project management, etc.

ME

MANY DISCIPLINES
Understanding & communications

MANY SYSTEMS
Understanding & communication

DEEP IN AT LEAST ONE DISCIPLINE
Analytic thinking & problem solving

DEEP IN AT LEAST ONE SYSTEM
Analytic thinking & problem solving

T-shaped Model

In the old hierarchical model, career steps progressed vertically and were reflective of differing levels of status: upwards from being a senior manager to a vice director to a director. The vertical was about developing a greater depth of knowledge in one subject and the assumption was the higher you went, the more experienced you were, but this is not always the case.

However, development along the horizontal matrix is hugely valuable, too, as it's about developing the breadth of understanding and connecting our expertise beyond our own speciality. The T part of the crossbar actually allows you to put that understanding into context and connect it to other people with different specialities. That's why we work as teams: because we can't do everything ourselves.

If you realise you have gaps in your knowledge related to complementary fields or have no idea what happens in your organisation

---

13 David Guest, 'The Hunt is On for the Renaissance Man of Computing', *The Independent* (17 September 1991).

after your contribution is complete, seek opportunities to expand your experience, like a new challenging project or a job rotation, and work in new areas. Like the bees, spend time in other areas of learning. I encourage you to get up and out of your jobs and join different community events or different networks. Move out of your comfort zone and into your learning zone.

If you are in a very focused, head-down role, take time to speak to people inside and outside of your industry. Speak to people in different career phases or on different paths. Be curious. When you look at other people's jobs, you are more aware of the bigger picture, and you begin to recognise what skills you will need for the future.

Don't leave this analysis to an annual performance review with your boss. That's a once-a-year, linear process. Take the initiative and create your own process of constant self-reflection and self-exploration to stay ahead of trends.

You may think all this continuous learning is obvious. Of course you need to stay ahead of trends and up to date. But have you considered your blind spots? We all have them. We all have assumptions and biases. Investigating our own blind spots and limitations in relation to learning is a crucial layer for personal and professional growth. It helps us avoid making faulty assumptions or judgements, leading to better decision-making and communication.

The Johari window is one psychological framework that can help us all better understand ourselves and our relationships with others. Developed in 1955 by American psychologists Joseph Luft and Harry Ingham, it remains highly relevant today.[14] It consists of four quadrants that represent different aspects of self-awareness which you can use to invite feedback, start conversations or initiate team-building exercises. (The name Johari comes from the authors' first names, Joseph and Harry.)

	Known to self	Not known to self
Known to others		
	Arena	Blind Spot
Not Known to others		
	Façade	Unkown

Johari Window

1. Open Arena: What you know about yourself and others. This includes behaviours, feelings and attitudes that are openly expressed and understood by everyone involved.

2. Blind Spot: What others know but you do not. These may be aspects of behaviour or characteristics that others can see but you may be unaware of.

3. Hidden Facade: What is known to you but not to others. Feelings, thoughts or experiences that are kept private and not shared openly with others.

4. Unknown Area: Information that is not known either to you or to others. It includes potential talents, traits or experiences that have not yet been discovered or explored.

---

14 Josesph Luft and Harrington Ingham, *The Johari Window: A Graphic Model of Interpersonal Awareness* (Los Angeles, CA: University of California/Western Training Lab, 1955).

When it comes to developing your learning, the Johari window is a good framework to use, as it encourages us to focus on what is hidden and unknown and to enhance leadership skills and communication.

To turn your research lens back on yourself is a difficult, scary and intimidating process. But it's important: your career is your responsibility, not the company's. Anita Rolls from the Career Intelligence Academy believes we all need to be the CEOs of our own career.[15] She reminds us that, like running a business, we need to work *in* our career as well as *on* our career. She proposes a model of four metaphorical hats we need to wear to drive our own career and lead a fulfilling life in today's changing world:

- The COO (Chief Operations Officer) Hat helps us to deliver value *in* our current role in a way that's sustainable and enjoyable for us too.

We also need to work *on* our career and make sure we make time for the following:

- The CFO (Chief Finance Officer) Hat helps us get clear on how we will measure success and what is most important to us in our career and life overall.
- The CMO (Chief Marketing Officer) Hat is all about showing up, not showing off – cultivating our brand and network based on who needs to know what we can and want to do.

---

15 Anita Rolls, 'Introducing Career Intelligence' [video], *YouTube* (uploaded 19 May 2021), https://www.youtube.com/watch?v=FT2ED9OmJvw, accessed 24 September 2024.

- The CIO (Chief Innovation Officer) Hat ensures we keep learning and developing our own valuable skills and capabilities, so we can keep reaching more of our potential and stay relevant to the needs of society and the the job market.

There is no longer such a thing as a job for life in a big organisation and if ever you have to leave that big organisation, it shouldn't come as a shock or a surprise.

Therefore, don't take anything for granted, don't stay static and don't assume the world's *not* changing. Be curious about what's going on for you as an individual; be curious about what's happening across society and in your industry. And keep being open-minded, keep learning and keep training.

Everything you know today you have learnt, and your potential to keep learning is limitless. The only barrier is a self-defeating belief that learning is no longer possible.

So, like the bees, keep moving. Keep learning. Keep adapting.

Response

by Katy Pountney to
Continuous Learning: A Worker Bee's Career

Katy is a human resources professional entering her third decade at a global pharmaceutical company based in Switzerland. Here, she enjoys the challenge of regularly reinventing organisations, teams and individuals, and not least her own contributions. Before that, having trained as a tax consultant, she worked as an HR consultant in the UK and Czech Republic.

In today's organisations, when even pension experts tell us to retire the concept of retirement, we know to take nothing for granted when it comes to planning our careers. But there are still reminders of those more predictable times. Of all the HR rituals in corporate life, perhaps 'talent reviews' are the most arcane. A group of 'elders' gather behind closed doors; curtains are pulled across glass walls and PowerPoint decks are marked 'strictly confidential'. 'Skills', 'potential', 'readiness', 'strengths' and 'growth areas': opinions are traded and compared like a human-sized game of Top Trumps.

Talent reviews were born in a world of more definable 'career ladders'. Together with their best friends, 'performance calibrations', they relied on shared, perhaps even quantifiable, definitions of success. These days, career experts advise us to think of our careers not as 'ladders', but as

Philip says, as a 'matrix' or even (the ultimate homage to a hive) as a 'honeycomb' where our paths can wind in all directions, no longer 'up or out'. Even more wildly, we're encouraged to think of our careers as a visit to a theme park: it's up to each of us to look out for the options all around us, choose the rides we want to go on, and know when it's time to get off and move on.

If we want to be ready for the theme park rides of the future, what skills should we be equipping ourselves with? The Center for Curriculum Redesign looked at the power Artificial Intelligence will bring, and the human skills required to harness it, and identified the following 'emphasis' areas: imagination, decision-making, dialogue, leadership, open-mindedness, risk-taking, resourcefulness, fairness and adaptability.[16] I find them a most optimistic and encouraging list of focus areas, and from my experience, I'd add two more: interdisciplinary knowledge (the ability to work between, and create dialogues across, our ever more specialised functions) and (inevitably) digital literacy. A call for lifelong learning that even a bee would be proud of.

Bees aren't the only career metaphors we can reach for though; perhaps they're not even the best example the animal kingdom has to offer. If we see our careers, not as ladders to climb, but as a series of experiences to learn and grow through, maybe lobsters can teach us a thing or two. In his renowned YouTube video, Rabbi Dr Abraham Twerski explains that the stimulus for a lobster to grow is a sense of discomfort.[17] As with the example of Philip's 'brilliant academic researcher', when we experience times of stress and adversity – or are wrestling with decisions around who we are and who we should become – we have just the right conditions to grow and, when the time is right, to shed our next layer.

---

16 Charles Fadel, et al., *Education for the Age of AI* (Boston, MA: The Center for Curriculum Redesign, 2024).

17 Rabbi Dr Abraham Twerski, 'On Responding To Stress' [video], *YouTube* (uploaded 26 Feb 2009), https://www.youtube.com/watch?v=3aDXM5H-Fuw&t=16s, accessed 24 September 2024.

Recommendations

If you're feeling like a moulting lobster, check out the work of Herminia Ibarra (her book, *Working Identity*,[18] or her articles and podcasts), who counsels that we figure out our transitions in the hustle of life through the trying and doing, not the thinking and planning (and certainly not relying on one of those talent reviews to show us the way).

Or if you have more to learn from the bees, fully immerse yourself in the transitions – and conflicts – of the hive by reading *The Bees*, the gripping 2014 novel by Laline Paull.

---

18 Herminia Ibarra, *Working Identity: Unconventional Strategies for Reinventing Your Career*, revised edition (Boston, MA: Harvard Business Review Press, 2023).

[6]

Decision-Making: The Swarm

The bees have their definite plan of life, perfected through countless ages, and nothing you can do will ever turn them from it. You can delay their work, or you can even thwart it altogether, but no one has ever succeeded in changing a single principle in bee-life. And so the best bee-master is always the one who most exactly obeys the orders from the hive.

— TICKNER EDWARDES, *The Bee-Master of Warrilow*, 1907.

In this chapter, we will dive deeper into the meaning of a swarm and the complex decision-making process that goes into one. Then we will apply this to our own decision-making skills and consider areas for improvement.

I F YOU'VE EVER SEEN a swarm of bees, it can be frightening. Tens of thousands of angry-sounding bees fly closely together through the air, then settle in an intimidating mass at about head height in a tree before moving to their new home. But I'd like to open your eyes to a different, more considered process that is happening.

Inside a hive, the queen has a main fertile period of two to five years. At the end of that period, the hive senses she is coming to the end of her useful power. (A bit like leaders at the end of a career phase.) The hive, as a collective unit, will decide it's time to generate a new queen, so they will feed the cells of female worker larvae with a special product called royal jelly: a powerful hormone that turns a regular female worker bee with a lifespan of a short month into a queen bee. She will be almost three times the size, with a longer lifespan, and will be exclusively dedicated to laying up to 2,000 eggs a day – that's more than her own body weight of eggs a day.

When an old queen is in a hive and a new queen is hatching, those two queens will need to fight or leave, and the members of the hive must choose which queen to support. It might be that the old queen fights a new queen, in which case one of them might die and the hive stays with the winner.

Or one queen might decide to leave and set up another colony, which will become their new home. This is how a colony reproduces. If that happens, 30,000 or so bees will need to decide what to do next: do they leave with the new queen and find a new place to live, with all of its inherent risks? Or do they decide to stay with the old queen in the old hive?

Bee Sex

A virgin queen will only make one flight in her life (unless she leaves with a swarm), called her honeymoon flight. She flies in a circle close to her hive in late spring. Male drones from her own hive or other hives will follow her, and she may mate with more than one drone while flying. The young queen's eggs are not fertilised straight away. She will store up to six million sperm from multiple drones in her spermatheca. When safely back in the hive, she will selectively release sperm to fertilise eggs for the remainder of her life. Those eggs that are fertilised become the female worker bees. Unfertilised eggs become the male drones. The male bees are therefore haploid, meaning they only have the genes possessed by the queen.

Choosing and travelling to a new home is not a decision the honey bees make lightly; for them, it's a life-or-death decision.

So how do these marvellous insects manage to successfully make such a big decision?

Within the hive, there are a number of scout bees. Scout bees will go off in multiple directions to look for a new home. If they find a place they recommend, they return as individuals and tell their colleagues what they have found through the process of the waggle dance. There might be many separate bees, each describing separate locations. Based on the scout bee's dance, the others will have to decide which of those new locations they are most curious about. Half a dozen or more bees might go to Site A, make their own interpretation and come back. Some other bees will follow a different scout bee, go to Site B and come back. The mass of bees will observe which bees are most committed to their opinion and how consistently and voraciously they communicate their energy for the site. This continues as a movement until there is a critical mass, such that the bees, as a majority population, have agreed on which swarming site they will go to.

When they're ready, they prepare to set off. They consume large quantities of honey to fuel their trip – so much so, the bees are actually rendered quite docile. So while a mob of thousands of swarming bees can look and sound quite terrifying, they are unlikely to sting you.

Through collective fact-finding, vigorous communication and consensus-building the bees are able to agree on a decision that will change the future of their hive.

Like humans, bees will never have perfect information but will collect more and more data until they have a consensus. Some of the scout bees, for example, will have found a suitable solution but will need to let it go to align with the consensus for the benefit of the hive.

What works well for bees can also work well for people. They have much to teach us when it comes to collective wisdom and effective decision-making. After all, bees are a complex social organisation, made of tens of thousands of individuals organised enough to make one decision they can all align behind. Wouldn't it be wonderful if we saw that in organisations and society today?

Decision-making by groups, whether by honey bees or humans, can often prove to be more fruitful than if the decision were made by the smartest individuals in that group. Unfortunately, that's not a common occurrence and we often see teams in an organisation paralysed by an inability to decide. Or they don't apply the appropriate decision-making process for the topic at that time. There are many decision-making frameworks to consider, including Herbert Simon's Satisficing model,[19] the Weighted Scoring model, de Bono's Six Thinking Hats,[20] the Kepner–Tregoe process[21] and the Cynefin framework.[22] For a team, it's helpful to be aware of and master a number of different models and

19 Herbert A. Simon, *Administrative Behavior: A Study of Decision-Making Processes in Administrative Organization*, 4th edition (New York: The Free Press, 1997).

20 Edward de Bono, *Six Thinking Hats* (Boston, MA: Little, Brown, 1985).

21 Kepner-Tregoe, https://kepner-tregoe.com, accessed 24 September 2024.

22 The Cynefin Company, https://thecynefin.co, accessed 24 September 2024.

be explicit and aligned on which approach is to be used. The goal is to ensure everyone can contribute productively.

One framework we can consider is decision-making by consensus, or by consent. Decision-making by consensus is where the majority (or everyone) has to align. It takes a lot of time and energy but it can be very fruitful, particularly for bigger, more strategic projects. Enough time needs to be allocated to this process in a team meeting's agenda, but with good facilitation it can be worth the effort. However, it is not always the most effective or efficient model to use.

Let's take an example of a leadership team I've been working with. Point one on their agenda was choosing a venue for the next conference. Five minutes were allocated to a packed agenda for the monthly leadership team meeting. All twelve highly-qualified people loved debating, discussing and sharing their ideas about which city to go to. Everyone had an opinion, and a marvellous time contributing, debating and disagreeing.

The topic took up a whole meeting, way exceeding the allotted time, and the conversation was completely irrelevant because no one really knew what the costs were, what the opportunities were and what the availability was.

A complete waste of time.

The team would do well in future to decide on what decision framework they're going to use and what category this decision falls into. Is it information sharing? Do we need to make a simple decision? Are we diving deeper into a topic that requires careful thought and discussion? These are three very different agenda items, each of which needs to be structured differently. In this situation, it would have been good to delegate and empower one or two team members to find the facts, evaluate the options and come back with a recommendation. If they need more data or more input, they are also empowered to seek whatever information they need. This is decision-making by consent: we trust you to decide.

We often see a leadership team meeting being held, with a long list of agenda items to tick off. However, each topic is allocated the same amount of time, the items are all dealt with in the same way and frequently, meetings don't finish on time because every topic requires a different process.

A leadership team was recently tasked with evaluating a number of proposals. It's easy for everyone to dive into every topic and to let the discussion spiral out of control. It's more efficient, however, to structure the meeting to hear from everyone in a disciplined way. One discipline we use is a bit like *Dragon's Den*.[23] People present their proposals, and we invite everyone in the meeting to share two things. The first is: 'What I like about the proposal.' And the second thing is: 'I would like you to consider the following.' And we go around the room as a discipline, where every member of the meeting follows that process to provide their input.

After the owners of the proposals have heard from everybody equally and everyone has had an equal voice and an equal contribution, then we invite the proposal owners to respond. There might be things they want to take away and develop. There might be things they've considered and dismissed. There might be things they've not considered at all. What a lovely, generative way to improve a proposal. One which takes a structure and a process.

Without this, you risk getting some overpowering individuals with strong opinions taking the conversation in a direction that might not

---

23 *Dragon's Den* [tv] prod. Darrell Olsen and Samantha Davies (televised by the BBC 2005–present).

be helpful. The conversation may have been triggered, steered and dominated by the same extrovert who always wants to share their opinions. You risk excluding other people's opinions, and other factors. Everything needs more conscious thought and more appropriate design. And fabulous facilitation superpowers.

Decision-making by consensus is not always necessary. Decision-making by consent is often a lot quicker, and a much better use of an organisation's management, time and resources. It's where you say, 'I trust you to decide on our behalf'.

If there is a budget decision, a resource decision or you need to choose a location for an offsite meeting, do you always need a team of all leaders working on that? 30,000 bees don't all go looking for a new hive site!

Don't waste time by involving more people than necessary. It's going to be more efficient to allocate a small working task force of two or three people. Like scout bees, let them go away, look at the alternatives, make a recommendation and bring that back to the group. Then use the power of collective thinking to assess the merit of the decision.

Trust those people to make a recommendation. This is not where you micromanage or try to take over the decision process. Give them the space and the accountability to do a good job, thereby saving time and using the collective wisdom of the crowd on the quality of the decision. If you've agreed on the important criteria before you start, acknowledge you will support the best recommendation the task force comes back with. Then a team can align to a single decision and agree to put their previous differences aside, like the swarming bees do.

If it's a more complicated decision requiring input from the whole group, then consciously label that as decision-making by consensus and allocate sufficient time for it. Save your experience, energy and superpowers for the big, important stuff, and when you do, agree on the models and frameworks you're going to use. That's why it can be invaluable to have a skilled professional facilitator to help drive the group to the right decision.

There is also a risk to be aware of, and that is making decisions based on the lowest common denominator.

If we think we know the answer, we often jump to a solution instead of expanding our knowledge, opening up and asking: 'What haven't we considered? What would we do in a different situation? What would the competitors do?' Engage in divergent thinking before coming to the convergent process of making a decision.

There's a terrible aphorism that goes: 'No one ever got fired for hiring IBM.' Just because it's industry standard doesn't mean it's a good decision. It doesn't mean it's the brave decision, or the most intelligent. Organisations and leadership teams often make a big decision because it's acknowledged as being a safe decision. But with a little bit of extra thinking and a little bit more courage and accountability, you might have come to a different decision better suited to the situation.

As with everything in life, but rarely seen in meetings, agree upfront about what type of decision-making model is going to be useful in any situation. It may be that you need to kick the bees' nest and explore more alternatives. Be open to investing time into looking at other options, thinking about what other industries might do, and encouraging divergent thinking. Spend more time opening up possibilities and understanding what the differences are and where your competitive advantage could be.

And then take a decision.

Celebrate it and move on.

Be just like the bees moving to a new home that is more fit for purpose.

Response

by Bernhard Sterchi to
Decision-Making: The Swarm

Bernhard has been called a thought sorter and player of Tetris with ideas. As managing partner of Palladio Trusted Advisers, he works as trainer, coach and consultant. He is the author of The Leader's Fairytales *and* Oblique Strategies for Leaders, *and creator of the Peerview App.*

What is a swarm? It is composed of many individuals, but at the same time, it has some kind of identity of its own. It *decides* to hatch a new queen. But then again, that decision is something quite different from a decision we make as individuals. It is more fragmented and incomplete. There is no central ledger of all bees and their 'vote' on a new location, no central knowledge that everyone has made up their mind, and yet there is a moment when 'deliberation' turns into action.

You can describe the swarm as an organisation: multiple individuals working together for a common purpose. Niklas Luhmann's work on social theory suggests three elements that distinguish an organisation from other social systems: purpose, hierarchy and membership.[24] I think that gives us a useful framework for decision-making. If an organisation has a common purpose, then by definition everything the organisation

---

24 Niklas Luhmann, *Social Systems*, trans. John Bednarz, Jr. (Stanford, CA: Stanford University Press, 1995).

does is pragmatic. The main criterion is how useful something is for the purpose. Bees have this pragmatism in their DNA. For us humans it is helpful to remind ourselves constantly to be pragmatic, making decisions based on a usefulness towards the purpose. No organisations have enough resources to put every good idea into practice. They need to make decisions to prioritise activities. In any organisation with division of labour, there are necessarily contradicting answers about how to prioritise. This is because best performance always happens in a local optimum: I do exactly what my customer needs. I choose the best solution to my problem. But to achieve the best performance for the whole organisation, you need cohesion. Customers should be treated according to the same standard. Synergies and efficiencies should play a role in the choice of solutions.

It is therefore essential for an organisation to be able to impose the logic of cohesion over the local logic, if necessary. But for performance, it is better to do as little as possible. Give as much autonomy as possible, within the boundaries of a hierarchy. Nobody tells the scout bees which destination to promote. But the swarm migrates to only one location, against the proposals of many individual scout bees.

The beehive also shows we are talking about a hierarchy of decisions, not of individuals. What is good for the whole can trump what is good for a part. Whether this happens by general assembly, networked negotiations, deliberations of experts or a single manager, is open to question.

There is only one condition to be respected. The amount of coordination and information work one needs before doing one's job, needs to be at human scale. If everybody needs to know what everybody else does so they can do their own job, the organisation will not perform. This is what fascinates me about the swarm's fragmented nature: nobody knows everything. And yet the swarm is capable of acting in cohesion.

The above framework gives a background to the chapter's conclusion:

it is helpful for a team to have a framework for their decision-making so they can choose in a pragmatic way what method works best to decide their specific case.

There are many useful decision frameworks to consider and also key questions for leaders and teams to ask themselves before rushing to make a decision.

Questions to ask at different phases of a decision-making process

- Analysing the situation:
  - How can we get the best information?
- What criteria the solution needs to fulfil:
  - Who is the client? Who gives the mandate? What are their needs?
- Searching many possible solutions:
  - How can we think out of the box? Who is creative? Who knows similar cases?
- Choosing the best solution:
  - Who bears the responsibility? Whose ownership do we need?
- Implementing the solution:
  - Who do we need on board? How do we involve them earlier?
- Managing the risks of the chosen solution:
  - Who are our warning sentinels? What are warning signs? How can we capture the weak signals?

There are a number of different decision-making frameworks that all have merit in different situations.

Dave Snowden's Cynefin framework[25] presents four domains

- In clear situations, categorise the problem and apply the respective measures.
- In complicated situations, analyse the problem with expertise and research.
- In complex situations, probe the system, explore and experiment with various approaches by trial and error, and scale what proves to be working.
- In chaotic situations, have some fire drill approaches ready that allow you to act fast, and then improve as you go along.

Edward de Bono's Six Thinking Hats is another interesting model to consider.[26] In my view, this is an example of how you can sequence a decision in a group, and thus make the deliberations independent of the individual participant's opinions. First, let's all find the advantages, then the disadvantages, then let's explore how the situation looks from a client's perspective, then from a financial perspective, etc.

The original Six Thinking Hats are:

1. Facts and information.
2. Optimism, benefits, advantages.
3. Risks, difficulties, problems.
4. Feelings, hunches, intuitions.
5. Creativity, possibilities, alternatives.
6. Managing the thinking process: what are we doing right now?

---

25 Cynefin, https://thecynefin.co.
26 de Bono, *Six Thinking Hats*.

Weighted scoring is a more quantitative approach. This can be a very helpful discipline when the pros and cons of various options with many features need to be compared. List your must-have requirements, followed by the optional requirements, assigning a weight (1–10) to the latter. Then draw out a table with your options and decide the satisfaction (1–10) of each option against each requirement. Multiply weight and satisfaction and draw a sum of that for each option. The sum does not dictate your choice but you can focus the discussion on the critical points: which weight and which satisfaction would tip the decision?

Another framework is Herbert Simon's Satisficing approach.[27] This applies to situations of bounded rationality, where various contradicting objectives or infinite opportunities cannot be put into one formula. Start with defining your aspirational level: what is the minimum necessary for a solution to work? Then go with the first option that satisfies these criteria. In short, it means to choose what's good enough instead of searching for what's best. An alternative is 'good enough to try'.

Like the bees, I hope you find the right process to make the right decision!

---

27 Simon, *Administrative Behavior*.

AUTUMN

Autumn in nature is a time of consolidation. Flowering plants and blossoms have already been fertilised and energy has been harnessed to produce fruits and growth. Inside a hive the worker bees prepare for the cold months of winter. Honey stores are matured and sealed. Precious resources are conserved – male drones are no longer useful and are expelled.

In organisations we are preparing for the year's end too. Annual targets need to be reached. Reviews and talent management planning must be prepared for.

In this section, we look at:

[7]

Teamwork:
Harvest Time

If you want to go fast, go alone; if you want to go far, go together.
— AFRICAN PROVERB.

In this chapter, we dive into the wonderful and sticky mess of harvesting honey. We know how bees work as a team to produce it, but let's look at how beekeepers need to work together to harvest it. Then I will share some reflections on teamwork in the working environment today and focus on one key factor that can increase team performance.

HOW YOU GET HONEY from a beehive closely guarded by 30,000 bees is actually quite a remarkable, beautiful and messy story. It's a time when you will really need support because this whole process cannot be done alone. It's a team effort, and you need to conscript willing family members, friends and neighbours to help.

Part of the problem is that a traditional honey box, sitting on top of a hive, can weigh upwards of 20 kilogrammes and it's always exactly the wrong height for your lower back, so you have to have a bee buddy to help (if not just to save the health of your back). I work with my dear friend Frank, and we share the beekeeping together.

The bees use bee glue, propolis, to reinforce the insides of a hive, seal any cracks and prevent draughts. Therefore, the first difficult task is to lever and separate the boxes of honey, the supers, to remove them from the main body of the hive where the queen is laying her eggs, and the worker bees are rearing the young. Once you and your bee buddy have removed these heavy honey-laden boxes and transported them to your car, you then need help carrying them into your home, and onto the kitchen counter. All while it begins to leak honey, and you have a small swarm of overexcited bees following you because they want their honey back.

Then, when you arrive at your kitchen table with a box of frames (ideally without an angry swarm of bees following you) you have to get the honey out by carefully decapping each cell. This means using a fine knife or special implement (invariably sticky) to shave the wax-sealed caps off each cell of honey without damaging the whole comb too much. It's a delicate and laborious job, and you need reinforcements. (I find four small children with good eyesight and small hands particularly well-suited to this job.)

Once you've done that you need to lift each frame into a honey-extracting machine. The one I have is a bit like an old-fashioned, hand-powered washing machine that takes up most of the open space in a kitchen. You hang eight to ten frames vertically inside a cylinder, and through centrifugal force and a lot of hard manual labour, you spin frames so runny honey is forced outwards to the vertical walls of the spinner.

Add to this the pressure of time. Honey is hydrophilic. It attracts moisture, which is why the bees keep the cells of mature honey capped with wax to create an airtight seal. By removing the wax cover, you are exposing the honey to moisture in the air. If it's a humid day and the honey goes above 18% moisture content, it may ferment quickly turning the sugars to alcohol, carbon dioxide and acetic acid. So the quicker you harvest, the better the honey. It's a wonderful feeling when you first open the tap at the bottom of the spinner and the honey runs out. It smells divine as you collect it in a bucket, seal it with an airtight lid and let it settle before decanting into jars.

But the work's not done yet.

Each frame of honey that has had its wax covers cut open and spun to remove the majority of the honey is a sticky mess. Some honey remains and these 'wet frames' must be quickly returned to the bees. They feast on what's left of their precious honey and put their energy into cleaning and repairing the cells with new wax, ready for new honey to be processed. A clumsy beekeeper may have caused significant damage to the cells and frames, which will be a big drain on a colony's time and resources to rebuild.

Once the whole process is complete and the matured honey is secured, there is an extensive clean-up process that involves washing sticky honey out of floors, walls and children's hair. This all needs doing before my wife returns! Many beekeepers around the world have a story about how when they were kids, they would help distant uncles, aunts and neighbours harvest their honey. I hear these stories all the time and it's always about the community feeling of beekeeping that's so lovely. Harvesting is a time when you really need some friends.

Business today is all about teamwork, too, but organisations are not always structured to support teamwork. The historical way of looking at organisations was as individuals in reporting lines, connecting you to a single leader above you. Appraisals were about individuals and goal setting. Individual bonuses and salaries. Individual behaviour. And for a long time, the focus has been on how to get the individual to work harder.

In organisations, however, nothing is done in isolation, and in business there are very few tasks where people can be the sole subject matter experts. Like a hive, each individual bee cannot survive or perform by itself; instead, it forms specialised groups. Nurse bees work together to feed the queen and security bees work as an efficient unit supporting each other. In organisations we all perform multiple roles within different groups of people, each of us dealing with varying levels of organisational tension: positive tensions that hold people together and corrosive tensions that push us apart.

A lot of the negative tension and frustrations in an organisation stem from its teams. Katzenbach and Smith indicate in *The Wisdom of Teams* that many teams are 'pseudo' in nature, in effect pretending to be a team but without delivering the promised performance output: the sum of the whole may be less than the potential of the sum of the parts.[28] Individuals or leaders may work within multiple teams at any one time, but just being part of a leadership team, and reporting to a more senior leader, doesn't always mean they are an actual team.

The traditional organisational approach assumes all teams are similar: facing the same issues and the same obstacles, requiring the same support and framework of leadership to reach high performance. But in reality, teams are much more nuanced. Therefore, my colleagues and I believe the focus should not be about individual success within a group but about the team as the unit of success. We no longer work in single production lines, reporting to one leader. Today, success comes

---

28 Jon Katzenbach and Douglas Smith, *The Wisdom of Teams: Creating the High-Performance Organization* (Boston, MA: Harvard Business Review Press, 1993).

from embracing a more flexible process where the lines of connection are more interwoven and layered than linear. Teams come together and separate depending on the need and the project.

And this is where it gets more complicated.

How do we define what a team is? How do we reward a team, and how do we reach high performance? To solve this, we need to redefine what a team is and my colleague, Dave Kesby, has identified two distinct types: an extra-dependent team and an inter-dependent team. Each type requires a different approach and level of management support. A deeper understanding of these two types will immediately help us locate the positive and negative tensions in our organisations, and once we understand what they are, we will be better positioned to lead. His work is published in *Extra-Dependent Teams: Realising the Power of Similarity.*[29]

Inter-dependent

An inter-dependent team is a bit like a soccer team where you have multiple people with multiple different skills, roles and functions working together to complete a common goal. In a business team, that might mean you have a business analyst, a market researcher, a finance person and so on.

If any one of those people is missing, for example, your goalkeeper or striker is absent, or your business analyst, you are exposed. An inter-dependent team relies upon the other members *in* their own team to be successful; they are INter-dependent. Having regular meetings and updates on the status of each project they are working on will be a valuable exercise. Most of us will be familiar with this well-known classic type of team, and most organisations will tend to assume all their teams are inter-dependent.

But that's not always the case.

---

29 David Kesby, *Extra-Dependent Teams: Realising the Power of Similarity* (London: Routledge, 2018).

Extra-dependent

Extra-dependent teams are ones where members depend on others outside of their team for their success. They all share a similar job role, they all report to the same manager, but they do not depend on each other for success and their work is delivered outside the remit of their group's leader. Extra-dependent teams can be prevalent in organisations. In one study of a multinational pharmaceutical company, we found that up to 50% of people were members of extra-dependent teams. A good example is a team of communication managers, who all perform a similar role delivering their work to different parts of the business: they leave the home team to go to their business partner's team to deliver their work and then come back again. Other examples include a region of sales managers, business analysts, midwives working in the community or a team of neighbouring priests in the same diocese. Organisations are less familiar with this concept of extra-dependent teams, which is why I want to focus more on this type. They require a specific awareness, leadership approach and actions.

Extra-dependent team meetings can be toxically boring and risk creating competition and negativity for its members. Early in my career as a sales representative, I remember a regional sales league table was shared at the beginning of each meeting. Instead of motivating me, it made me feel insecure and competitive. When holding extra-dependent team meetings, there's no point in sharing an update of each of your individual projects because they're not going to be relevant to the other team members. If attendance is dropping it will be because extra-dependent team members are prioritising the meetings of their client group, where they feel there is more value.

When I met Dave Kesby and read his book, I was leading a new team of communication managers. Sometimes it felt like herding cats! A light bulb went on for me and it helped me realise that leading an extra-dependent team requires a different mental framework to support and develop them.

In the book, he suggests a better use of time for extra-dependent teams would be to come together to improve techniques and to share learnings and skills, rather than to compare project results. Team members will have more to gain from leadership team meetings when they are hubs of learning and growth, advice and support, rather than a microcosm of internal competition. For the leader, this lifts the performance of each individual and as a result the whole group.

Of course, all of this requires good facilitation and a high level of trust and psychological safety, which leads me to the next point.

Just like harvesting honey together, all team members must play their part and contribute fully. To fully contribute though, each team member needs to feel 'safe' to do so without fear of retribution. The sense of safety and willingness to speak up is not an individual trait, however, and even though it's something you do feel and experience at the individual level, it's an emergent property of the group.

Amy Edmondson is the Novartis Professor of Leadership and Management at Harvard Business School. In her book, *The Fearless Organization*, she shares the results of a study into the relationship between error-making and teamwork in hospitals.[30] She expected to find that more effective teams make fewer mistakes. But conversely, it was the teams who experienced more errors that reported better teamwork – higher-performing teams were more willing to report their mistakes

---

30 Amy C. Edmondson, *The Fearless Organization: Creating Psychological Safety in the Workplace for Learning, Innovation, and Growth* (Hoboken, NJ: John Wiley & Sons, Inc., 2018).

because they felt safe doing so. Teams that had worse performance actually felt less safe to declare their mistakes so data was not recorded.

In 2012, the leadership team at Google initiated Project Aristotle to identify the key factors that make a successful team. Julia Rozovsky and her team of researchers originally thought diversity or a team's demographics would have the biggest impact, but after analysing vast amounts of data, the project concluded that who was on a team mattered less than *how* the team worked together, and psychological safety was the most important factor for team success. There's no point in hiring one of the greatest computer scientists into an organisation and a leadership team if they don't feel safe to speak up and contribute fully.

Psychological safety is therefore a critical concept for teams and the people who lead them. Team psychological safety is especially important because it is a group-level phenomenon – it shapes the learning behaviour of all members and in turn, affects team performance and by extension, organisational performance.

Psychological safety leads to team members feeling more engaged and motivated, as they feel their contributions matter and they're able to speak up without fear of retribution. It can lead to better decision-making, as people feel more comfortable voicing their opinions and concerns, which often leads to a more diverse range of perspectives being heard and considered. Finally, it can foster a culture of continuous learning and improvement, as team members feel comfortable sharing their mistakes and learning from them.

So, how do you know your team is psychologically safe? A likely question on many leaders' minds. Edmondson has developed a simple seven-item questionnaire to assess the perception of psychological safety. How people answer these questions will give you a sense of the degree to which they feel psychologically safe:

1. If you make a mistake on this team, it is not held against you.
2. Members of this team are able to bring up problems and tough issues.
3. People on this team accept others for being different.
4. It is safe to take a risk on this team.
5. It isn't difficult to ask other members of this team for help.
6. No one on this team would deliberately act in a way that undermines my efforts.
7. Working with members of this team, my unique skills and talents are valued and used.

Your role as the team leader is to better understand the whole system and to create the right environment for each team member to flourish, and create connections and relationships. Not to get in the way.

Understand what type of team you are leading, hire brilliant people and let them be brilliant. Trust your team. And if you find you can't, that's something to stop and think about.

The feedback could be stinging.

Response

by Dave Kesby to
Teamwork: Harvest Time

Dave is an experienced executive and team coach who authored Extra-Dependent Teams: Realising the Power of Similarity. *He is the founder of Organisational Coaching Hub, which provides coaching capabilities to organisations, teams and individuals. He is driven by his purpose that 'Everyone deserves to be led well'.*

A hive must be full of teams! Think of the thousands of individual bees that make up a colony.

Teams are the middle ground between individuals and organisations. Of course teams consist of individuals, but together as a team, those individuals are so much more. Teams have their own dynamics, purpose and identity – on top of those of individuals. It's not just a series of 'I's'. Teams are best considered as a single unit rather than lots of individuals. And the best teams recognise they are part of the organisation, with multiple stakeholders they interact with, many of which are other teams. The organisational system is a mass of overlapping, interlocking and interconnecting teams: a team of teams; a colony.

Philip and I both love the connectedness of teams and the power they bring. Indeed, as he handed me his draft, it didn't feel right to just go ahead and write something – however urgent the deadline was! Instead, I emailed Philip some questions and he responded immediately by calling me. Email has its place but teaming often requires quality dialogue and Philip's hive mentality defaulted to a richer form of communication. We talked things through and shared some feedback. As a result, we finished feeling more enabled than when we started. It was a lovely illustration of synergy – the whole being greater than the sum. This is what teaming is all about and this is what I love about working with Philip, other colleagues and teams.

We think teaming is simple. It's not. If it was, then why would Harvard professors such as Amy Edmonson and huge organisations such as Google still study teams and find new insights? I imagine teaming within a hive isn't simple either. Indeed, the more I've learned about hive life from Philip, the more complex I realise it is.

Perhaps this is a useful way for us to recognise the complexities of teams. To permit ourselves to be more curious about what's really going on. Before I started learning about bees from Philip, I could easily have oversimplified a hive as a box where bees turn nectar into honey. That description is right enough to spot one in a field. But if I was a farmer or a beekeeper, it just isn't enough because they depend on what the bees do.

In my experience, many managers see teams in the same way I used to see hives: an oversimplification of a complex dynamic that interacts with the ecosystem. Led well, the team generates wonderful results whilst giving and taking enough to be sustainable.

To lead well requires a greater appreciation of what's going on in the hive – in the team. When you start to learn about teams, when you really notice what's going on, leadership transforms from being a list of tasks into something more like beekeeping: a craft that combines care, attention and a willingness to respond in the moment to what the bees need. Mastering this craft takes study, practice and desire. That's why I continue to be fascinated by teams, and I encourage managers and team members alike to be fascinated too.

When I ask people to define a team, about nine times out of ten they answer along the lines of 'a group of people all working together to achieve a common goal'. This oversimplification leads us to want what we don't see and miss what we actually see. Many teams are set up to work together, but many others are simply not. It's these teams I've been particularly fascinated with over the years as they are often treated as dysfunctional because everyone is acting individually. When you really pay attention, however, it's easy to notice that actually, they are perfectly OK. That's because they do a different type of teaming within the wider organisation. I call them extra-dependent teams because they depend more on people outside than inside. As a result, they are fundamentally different from inter-dependent teams. All too often it's not the teams that are dysfunctional, but the leadership.

Just like the reality of bees in a hive, who would have thought there were different types of bees? Or that they conducted different roles? And that these roles changed over the seasons? And who would have thought that in organisations there are different types of teams?

I invite you to look around your organisation to find the teams where members do similar work but do that work outside the team. When you find them it's a bit like realising there are different types of bees in a hive. Once you know they exist, not only do you start to notice them but you realise their contribution is vital within the wider organisation. Extra-dependent teams often consist of specialists who add great value to other, often inter-dependent teams, but mostly individually. Leaders of inter-dependent teams need to incorporate these individual contributors into their teams as they depend on their specialisms. And leaders of extra-dependent teams need to encourage their members to be more than their specialism – to be active team members outside their team.

Which type of teams have you been a member of? What oversimplifications of teams have you been working with? What are you now more curious about as you start to notice more about what's really going on in teams?

Change and Diversity: Responding to the Environment

There are not more than five musical notes, yet the combinations of these five give rise to more melodies than can ever be heard. There are not more than five primary colours ... yet in combination they produce more hues than can ever be seen. There are not more than five cardinal tastes ... yet combinations of them yield more flavours than can ever be tasted.

– Sun Tzu, *The Art of War.*

Autumn is a time of great change. As our days get shorter and the temperature begins to fall, we will think about how bees adapt to their environment and what we can do to support them. We will look at an example of bees around the world, and reflect on the importance of supporting individual changing needs and creating space for diversity to flourish.

O N A RECENT TRIP TO THE MIDDLE EAST, a colleague took me to a local market. On an amazingly hot evening under the stars, we stopped at a honey stall. In between the displays of figs and fruit, spices and herbs, was an old man with multiple open jars of different types of honey. The world over, honey sellers are proud of their precious products and this man was no different. My colleague explained to him that I was a beekeeper back in Europe and his face beamed. He encouraged me to dip a wooden spoon into a small jar to taste the sweet, sticky, delightful product. My curiosity about all things bees and honey in this desert environment was piqued. I learned the local bees (Apis florea) are a lot smaller than those we may see in Europe, smaller than the nail on our little finger, and a dark red-brown colour. I learned that due to extensive urbanisation, these wild honey bees native to the Middle East region are losing their natural habitat; the edges of deserts where the scrub and flowers usually grow are disappearing. Consequently, during swarming season, these small and dark honey bees often land on people's balconies in high-rise apartments to rest. Sadly, the first reflex of their unexpecting human hosts is to call pest control, and that means the inevitable killing of a colony or of individual bees.

It's all well and good having irrigated and intensive farming, but you still need bees to pollinate your crops. So, while there is some wild honey produced in the region, the majority of commercial pollination and honey production comes from imported queens of the honey bees we know well, the Apis mellifera, also known as the Western honey bee. About half a million packaged honey bee colonies are shipped every year from Egypt, Oman and Yemen into the United Arab Emirates. Even so, these imported Western honey bees are not a perfect solution. They are not equipped to survive the harsh climate or the shortage of foraging plants that occur naturally beyond intensive agriculture and need to be looked after carefully if they are to survive.

Bees, whether native or imported, all bring value to our greater ecosystem and it's important to be aware of their different needs in order to get the best from them. For the imported migrant bees to thrive it is essential to support them. In the United Arab Emirates, careful beekeepers will move their hives of Western honey bees into the cooler Hajar Mountains to ensure the bees' survival as the temperature rises. If a struggling bee lands on your high-rise building balcony or windowsill, it will only want a plate of water and sugar to fuel it on its way. It is not there to sting you. And if a swarm arrives, they are only thinking of survival and will soon move to a place that suits them. They are far from wanting to cause harm; they are just doing their best to adapt to the current difficult environment so they can do their best work. Calling pest control at the first sighting of an unfamiliar bee on your balcony is a direct consequence of a fear of what we don't understand, and a lack of information and understanding of a bee's important role in our world.

If you see a strange coloured bee, be it big, black and yellow or tiny, dark and red-brown, there is no need to panic; we're all on the same side. What the bees really need is some love and support. And with careful management and care the bees can survive.

So I say, long live the bees, wherever they are in the world.

Whether you're working in the Middle East or anywhere else in the world, diversity of experience, opinion and thought contributes to a better outcome. Hopefully, the working world has made good progress in terms of diversity. However, potential employers are still falling short and the board commitment or metrics for diversity may not be sending the right message.

In an impactful article from the *Harvard Business Review* in 2022, authors Oriane Georgeac and Aneeta Rattan suggested company boards should stop making a business case for diversity, equity and inclusion

(DEI).[31] Companies don't feel the need to explain why they believe in values such as innovation, resilience or integrity, so why treat diversity any differently?

Eighty per cent of Fortune 500 companies justify diversity in the workplace because it benefits their bottom line. And yet, the authors found this approach actually makes underrepresented job candidates a lot less interested in working for an organisation. This is because the rhetoric that makes the business case for diversity sends a subtle yet impactful signal that organisations view employees from underrepresented groups as a means to an end, ultimately undermining DEI efforts before employers have even had the chance to interact with potential employees.

Based on their findings, the authors suggest that if organisations must justify their commitment to diversity, they should do so by making an argument based on moral grounds.

If we want to encourage more diverse opinions and thought, we have a responsibility to design processes and interventions that cater for this outcome and change the rhetoric. Employing people from underrepresented groups is not a means to an end or a box-ticking exercise. It is essential to reflect the needs of a diverse society and to optimise how we think and behave as a team.

There are many forms of diversity to consider and be aware of beyond gender, race and sexuality. Let's look at factors of neurodiversity, for example. People have fundamentally different styles for how they think and engage with data, each other, and the world. In Susan Cain's

---

31 Oriane Georgeac and Aneeta Rattan, 'Stop Making the Business Case for Diversity', *Harvard Business Review* (15 June 2022).

book, *Quiet: The Power of Introverts in a World That Can't Stop Talking*, she makes a case for leaders to make space for differing thinking types within a team.[32] Everyone should feel safe to speak up, to feel heard and to contribute.

However, workplaces and meetings are rarely designed to support different thinking styles. We often witness a situation where the extroverts are delighted to have an audience before which to show their prowess, and in a meeting, they can't wait to put their hand up and speak. We all know they're extroverts because they start speaking without knowing what the end is going to be, and that's a lovely gift; let's celebrate it. But let's also make time for the introverts who need time to think and process, before contributing optimally. We all want to engage in a way that allows us to be at our best, and that needs to be acknowledged.

If you want to design a meeting so it's a comfortable place for every-one to contribute equally, one thing you can do is offer a mix of working methods and ways of gathering input. When collaborating online we often use the 1-2-4 model from Liberating Structures.[33]

We give space for each person to spend a moment reflecting on a question, then we suggest using breakout rooms where people can talk and work in pairs first, before bringing them together in larger groups of fours. And then, eventually, the full team can work together once a higher degree of psychological safety has been established. In this way, people at different points on the extrovert-introvert spectrum will each have a more equal opportunity during a single meeting to work in a way that benefits them.

You can also use the chat function in a more considered way. Typ-ically, the extroverted person might be the first to write and send a

---

32 Susan Cain, *Quiet: The Power of Introverts in a World That Can't Stop Talking* (London: Penguin Books, 2013).

33 Liberating Structures provide a selection of thirty-three alternative structures for facilitating meetings and conversations, curated by Henri Lipmanowicz and Keith McCandless. https://www.liberatingstructures.com, accessed 24 September 2024.

comment in the chat box, with everyone else being influenced to follow their lead. Instead, before writing anything, we encourage *everyone* to take a moment to think uninterrupted (which is important for introverts). Then everyone is asked to type their comment into that chat – without pressing send – giving time for everyone to think and write their considered response. Everyone then counts to three and all press 'send' together. That way no one is influenced by what the noisiest and quickest person has said. You get a huge rush of varied, unbiased data from different people, and that is the power of working as a diverse team with a higher level of trust.

If we're brainstorming ideas or taking part in long workshops, it's important to acknowledge people will work at different paces and manage their energy in different ways too. As well as considerations for introverts or extroverts, and those on the spectrum of neurodiversity, we should also pay attention to different learning styles. Some people prefer visual methods of learning, some prefer auditory, while some do their best when reading and writing are involved. Others may be more kinaesthetic and need to physically process the data.

The classic text, *Adult Learning Principles* by Catherine Mattiske, provides great insight that can help design adult learning interventions according to these specific needs.[34] If you are curious about your own preferred learning style and have never had time to stop to think about this (ahem) there are good online tools to help you.

We all have a predominant style that works best for us, and you may already know what works well for you. Take time to reflect on what

---

34 Catherine Mattiske, *Adult Learning Principles 1: Understanding the Ways Adults Learn*, 3rd edition (TPC – The Performance Company, 2011).

study methods you find the most effective and how you are best able to concentrate. For example, if you find reading over your notes from a textbook helps you prepare for a test, you might be a reading/writing learner or if you prefer to doodle and draw images or mind maps you may be a visual learner.

My daughter, for example, doesn't look at the school blackboard because visual data is too overwhelming. She's a kinaesthetic learner. She learns by moving. She counts things on her fingers and she's a fidget. She also has strong auditory learning tendencies, but she's not visual. If her teacher is presenting from the front of the class, my daughter will look out the window, listen intently and she may fidget, but she is most certainly learning.

For us as adults, it's just the same. I have heard of other organisations making space for kinaesthetic learners – in one case, welcoming an individual to knit a hat during team sessions. The movement of her hands and fingers helped her to concentrate and process the data. Another participant was able to spend certain parts of the session with her eyes closed, appearing deep in sleep, though as an audio learner she was fully engaged.

It's important to acknowledge and give space for all of these different behaviour types and to invite people to share, in a safe way, what they need to do to be at their best when hosting a meeting or collaborative activity. Make sure you're not organising training where people sit still in a room for hours without some variation of input and data processing. Create breakout sessions and opportunities for auditory processing, visual presentations or time for reading and writing. All facets of diversity are essential in modern working life and if we are to create success for ourselves and the organisations we work for, we need to acknowledge and put that into action.

Although the work we do at Hive-Logic is primarily for multinational companies based in Switzerland, we work with global organisations with a fascinating mix of people from different cultures. It means they might have different religious identities with different recognised feast days, holidays and celebrations. What a lovely opportunity to learn about the world around a single dining table when we are together in person, or what a fun opportunity to learn about the world in a single Zoom meeting!

It also means that while the language we work in, more often than not, is English, it's very rarely everyone else's first language. Let's not forget that if people have to translate their native language into English before they speak, they are working twice as hard as native English speakers in the room. So, let's create ways of working to ensure English speakers with their English idiosyncrasies and humour don't run away with the discussion.

We supported one very good leader who used to work in Argentina. When he came to his first head office role in Switzerland, he faced an unexpected challenge. A lot of the Argentinian patterns of behaviour, which had served him well, no longer worked. Particularly not in a global environment with people from twelve other nationalities. Even the concept of physical space was confusing. A 2017 study in the *Journal of Cross-Cultural Psychology*[35] identified that in Argentina, the average acceptable physical space between people is 76 centimetres for a colleague and 40 centimetres for a close friend. In the UK, we like to protect more of our own space with a comfortable distance of a metre and just over 50 centimetres for a close friend. Whilst Argentinians have

35 Agnieszka Sorokowska, 'Preferred Interpersonal Distances: A Global Comparison', *Journal of Cross-Cultural Psychology*, 48(4) (March 2017). DOI: http://dx.doi.org/10.1177/0022022117698039.

the smallest personal space, Romanians have the largest, preferring to keep 1.3 metres from someone they've just met. It's details like this that need to be recognised and as individuals, you cannot assume we all have the same set of physical, emotional or intellectual needs.

This particular leader couldn't understand why life was so difficult at first, but with good thought, good support and a willingness to be coached and to learn, he did well. But it took him far longer to adapt to this new environment than he was expecting.

So, please, new leaders reading this book, pay attention to this: it's easy to have a conformity bias with people of our own home country. It's very easy to form an allyship with people with whom we share a common culture or a common home language. But that in itself can be an obstacle to psychological safety for everyone within a team. Let's take time to learn and understand how each individual in our teams will be able to make their best contribution and then provide the right supportive environment for them to do that.

These are not just rules for working in global organisations; these are rules for life. Not just for leaders at work, but as parents, neighbours, sons, daughters and friends. This is about being a good global citizen, and as citizens of our own communities we all have this responsibility to acknowledge and recognise what we have in common.

Although there may be differences in how we process data or communicate, we all have similar goals and the very same hopes and fears. We're all on the same side.

While we might have been brought up with, or experienced, outdated models of working or opinions that were formed generations ago, these are the prejudices, biases and discriminatory beliefs that need challenging and stopping – actively.

In our role as leaders, we need to be ambassadors for change and make a strong stand against perpetuating those unhelpful stereotypes, myths and behaviours that have no place in a multifaceted, forward-thinking organisation and in our global world today.

All bees, whether the smaller Dwarf Honey Bee, Apis florea, or the larger European Honey Bee, Apis mellifera, make a vital contribution to the environment and life on our planet.

Response

by Jacqueline Rosenberg to
Change and Diversity: Responding to the Environment

Jacqueline is an organisation development, change and inclusion leader with a long career in the life sciences sector. She also has significant experience in market research, policy and consulting across the private, public and non-profit sectors. She is a behavioural scientist with a PhD in Health Behaviour Change.

Many organisations today are grappling with diversity, equity and inclusion (DEI). How can they embrace it? Should they set targets? How do they articulate it, internally and externally? And the challenge in many organisations is how to turn an attractively-laminated card displaying these kinds of lofty aspirations into something that's lived, real and sustainable.

Organisations often claim to value DEI but until it's a lived reality, a lived set of behaviours, then it's 'all mouth and no trousers', as we say. I've seen the ineffective and sometimes damaging effects of box-ticking Philip refers to in this chapter. While the intent may be positive, it is not particularly effective. There are some visible and invisible differences to consider, and that's quite an important distinction.

In Switzerland, for example, national service is a requirement for men but not for women. It can be military or civil service, but what this means in Switzerland – certainly historically, and still to an extent today – is that an invisible social network is built amongst men that helps them in their careers. It continues to play out in the working environment, and it's something women don't have access to and can't benefit from. So at least in Switzerland, that's quite a pervasive facet of inclusion, or exclusion, depending on your perspective, that is often invisible.

An example of an external, observable difference can be skin colour. Take me, for example. I'm white and that means I'm a member of a dominant group in the country I live and work in. I can agree or disagree that it's dominant, and I can agree or disagree with how marginalised people are treated. I can march as an ally and do all the work. But at the end of the day, however much I agree or disagree with the privileges white people have, I still benefit from them. You can be a man who is absolutely an ally for women in the workplace or supports equal pay, but you as a man are still benefiting from the privileges that are given to you through no fault or will of your own.

There is power in being part of a dominant group, whether that membership is visible or invisible, and we must all recognise that the dominant group sets the rules because the dominant group is in power (or in a seat of power, or in a leadership role). Being part of a dominant group means you get privileges. Whether you realise it or not.

Gender, age, sexual orientation, skin colour, handedness, religion, education, language and able-bodiedness are all examples of groups that will have a dominant group and a minority group.

One of the privileges of belonging to a dominant group (whether you have chosen to be part of it or not), is that your organisation is more likely to have your back. You are more likely to benefit in terms of your career; you will move through the organisation more easily as it works for you.

However, change happens when those with social organisational power have the self-awareness to realise they are part of the dominant group. And that means they can choose to change the rules to create power with and for, rather than maintain power over, people or groups.

For example, if you are invited to be a panellist at a conference, you can ask who else is on the panel. What will your response be if the answer is that they're all men? What do you say if they're all privately-rather than state-educated? What do you say if they are all native English speakers?

After all, representation matters: you have to see it to be it. Many organisations still have an underrepresentation of marginalised or minority groups, particularly in senior leadership, so when you're hiring, when you host an event, when you do anything, can the audience (or job applicant or guest panellist) see themselves represented in the company? If I'm from a disadvantaged, underserved community and the interviewing panel sounds like they've all been to private schools, am I going to think that's the place for me? And, even if I get a role, is that the place where I'm going to thrive?

DEI is also very multilayered. If you are a person of colour and you're a female, you will have a different experience to someone who is male and of colour, or female and white. What does that kind of layered experience mean for you? And the people you lead?

DEI goes back to self-awareness and knowing our own biases, conscious or unconscious, which can hinder everything from job postings, interview questions and performance reviews to project assignments. When I'm writing a job advert, I can ask myself: am I using inclusive language? Am I using words like 'driven' or 'fearless' or 'competitive' that male candidates tend to be more comfortable with? Or are there words that are more neutral that may encourage all applicants?

When working in global organisations and thinking about language, there also tends to be a bias towards English being the dominant language. But for people who have English as a second, third or fourth language, they might need a little more time to gather their thoughts before jumping into groups. Build in five or ten minutes before a brainstorming contribution in a team meeting (even if it seems uncomfortably long) for everybody to gather their thoughts.

Diversity in the workplace is a multifaceted topic, and the most important thing leaders can do is to recognise if they are part of a dominant group. If they are, I recommend they begin to build that self-awareness, own that group membership and use it responsibly. And if you are part of a minority or marginalised group in the workplace, form or join an employee resource group to provide support and advocacy, including working towards sustainable, inclusive policies. Sponsorship and mentoring programmes can also help with professional development and networking.

[9]

Sensing the System:
Avoid Being Stung!

*Leaders who refuse to listen will soon find themselves
surrounded by people with nothing to say.*

– ANON.

*In this chapter, we think about a beekeeper's relationship with their hive and
how using all our senses can help us to become better at our work. Let's look
at how this relates to our relationships in organisations. I will then share some
ideas and advice on becoming more in tune with our senses and about the whole
ecosystem of modern working life.*

BEES ARE NOT DANGEROUS. Inexperienced beekeepers are!
It's easy to march purposefully towards a beehive, to wade
in with our expertise and arrogance, and assume we know
what we're doing.

One evening, as a naive and arrogant young beekeeper, I did just
that: 'I'm just gonna have a quick look at my bees,' I told my son.

'Papa, you're wearing shorts, sandals and a t-shirt …'

'It's fine, Louis,' I said. 'I'll be fine. I work with the bees all the time. I'm on their side.'

It was not fine.

The bees did not want to work with me.

I got stung by one bee. Then I got stung by a second bee. Bees got up my shirt and buzzed furiously about my head.

I had to run down the street, flinging my clothes off as I fled the onslaught.

'Told you so.' Louis grinned after we were safe in the car and had closed the windows against the persistent and angry bees. He was right. I hadn't taken the time to assess the situation and be sure my presence was welcome or indeed, useful.

I hadn't stopped to appreciate what else was happening.

What I had failed to notice was that although it was a beautiful summer's evening, bathed in warm light and with a clear sky, wisps of cloud were forming on the horizon: a summer storm was brewing.

The bees could sense the dip in atmospheric pressure and were busying themselves to protect their hive. They had stopped their happy industry of foraging and making honey and had started making propolis, the bee glue they use to seal their hive.

I had underestimated how capable the bees were.

After all, they are the subject matter experts. They know perfectly well what's going on and they don't need anyone to step in and fix them, or make them better. Yes, as their beekeeper I wanted to get something from them – the honey or to check on their well-being – but the bees don't need me. They are working quite well without someone from head office interfering with them. I've now learned to approach the bees slowly, to pause and stop and notice what is happening by using all of my senses.

If you're ever near a hive, the first thing you will see is the activity, and the bees coming and going through the front door. When bees leave the hive, they don't fly very far: maybe less than a foot. Then they fly vertically, lifting high above the hive before setting off on their journey. If you see this flight pattern, that's a good sign. That's normal flight behaviour.

Then, as you get a bit closer you can hear the noise they're making. It's a lovely, reassuring hum that will be around 73 decibels and a frequency of 250 hertz. It's essentially the combined beating of 30,000 bees' wings and it has a musical tone of something like E flat. If the bees are stressed – if there's a storm coming for example – then it's a different tone: a higher pitch. You can hear they are stressed. But only if you stop and pause to listen …

The final sense you should use is your sense of smell. On a warm summer's day, as you approach the hive, you can smell it too. It's a lovely aroma of warm wax and rich honey. If you can smell that, you know they're doing the right things.

If the bees are stressed, if they are preparing for danger or in protection mode, against incoming bad weather for example, you can smell the production of propolis, a bee glue. It has a characteristic bitter smell – very different to honey, wax or flowers.

When we slow down, pause and use all our senses to gather information we can read the signs and know when it's safe to approach, so don't ignore what the system is telling you. If the bees are angry, you are significantly outnumbered, so don't go near them. Don't take the lid off, don't get out of the car; keep your distance. If the bees are happy, you're not going to get stung; you can go so far as to scoop up a handful of bees in your bare hands and you'll never get hurt, even if you're wearing shorts and sandals.

When we work with a team of subject matter experts, our goal as a leader is to drive a project forward and make it a success. We use the rational and logical parts of ourselves to achieve that as they serve us well. But how we work is even more important.

It's the *how* that is the differential between average performance and high performance. And that comes down to emotional intelligence. A lot of our work at Hive-Logic is around supporting leaders to lean into and increase their level of emotional awareness because as humans, we are not rational. We are not always logical. We are emotional beings driven and motivated by some very profound and important emotions like fear and anxiety. We also have aspirations, dreams and intuition.

So, while there is very much an intellectual component to the work we do, we mustn't forget the emotional and somatic elements. It's about how we connect as humans. We used to call it 'soft skills', but I think the very word 'soft' underplays the importance of them. In the work my colleagues and I do, we prefer to call them 'core skills' because they are fundamental and underpin everything else we do and experience. Having compassion and empathy, and being able to use all our senses, is essential to developing and increasing our emotional intelligence. So, let's think about these soft skills and how we can improve them in our own work.

Listening

In life, we don't do much listening. We may feel like we get paid to talk and to broadcast. That is what is acknowledged and rewarded. Journalists get paid by the word; barristers get paid by the hour. We measure the metrics of noise and volume, but not of silence and thought. Reflecting on the UK government during Prime Minister's Question

Time, the conversations are rarely about evoking a greater understanding or greater insight.

Sometimes people listen to interrupt: we focus on ourselves over what is being said.

Sometimes people listen to understand: we focus on the other person with curiosity.

What we should all aspire to is something deeper, where listening means to understand the greater context, the broader system and the environment we're operating in is taken into consideration and deeper thought is required: what other data is there to consider? What's happening between the lines? What are they not saying? These types of listening can be categorised as level one, level two and level three listening, respectively. If we pay more attention, we may see a great deal of incongruence, where people say one thing at a superficial level but their body language is saying something else. A good level three listener (and leader) will be able to pay deeper attention and notice any lack of congruence between body language and words. What is not said will often provide greater insight than what is verbalised.

We do an exercise in our training courses where we get people to work in pairs, each listening to the other person for four minutes and thirty-three seconds without interrupting. Nothing is said by the listener at all. It's a practice in listening and it's fascinating to notice what the other person will say in less than five minutes. If you ask someone how they are, the immediate reactive answer may be, 'I'm fine, thanks. I'm busy'. But given the freedom of four and a half minutes to talk, it's amazing what people reveal, just through the power of silence and good listening.

Side Note

Why four minutes and thirty-three seconds? In 1952, the contemporary composer John Cage wrote a modernist piece of music called *4'33"*. It is written to be played by a full orchestra and has been performed countless times in all the great major concert halls by the world's greatest symphony orchestras. If you held the musical score in your hand you would see no notes. No time signature. Nothing. It's fascinating. The conductor will stand up, the orchestra will prepare, and the audience will quiet down. And together they listen to silence for four minutes and thirty-three seconds. People come to the performance or buy the record because every single time it's different. People shuffle, people cough, people sneeze. You can hear birds outside. Something special happens just by listening to silence. And it makes people think. It creates a thought. And, for me, the definition of good art is that it makes people think.

Somatic

Somatic means relating to, or affecting, the body, which is a concept that is even less embraced and discussed at work. I use it here to bring in the concept of 'gut feeling' and intuition but also to consider how we physically present ourselves at work. You need to work with congruence such that your words, your actions and how you deliver your message are all consistent. Using your intuition – your gut feeling – is about being more aware of what your body is saying. So, let's look at these two separately: the body and the gut.

First, the body. We all know colleagues who anxiously tap their foot. Or we call it a 'sewing machine knee' when someone's knee goes up and down, and in person you could notice that in a meeting and feel annoyed.

But what it's telling you is that there is trapped energy that's not being released. It might be a tell that there's emotion inside that person they're not able to express verbally: frustration, anger or something deeper. It's a body communicating what it's feeling, and it needs to be thought about.

Now, if you're on a virtual call, you can't see if someone's knee is tapping, but if you look closely there will be clues. You might notice there is some element of pent-up energy through the way people speak, or how they glance at the clock a few too many times. A shorter than normal answer. Or a feeling of disengagement.

In the next video call, try looking at how people position their heads. Sometimes we see people sitting back. Of course, that's a classic position and won't always mean anything, but occasionally people move away from the screen to protect themselves or to shut down. When people are in a pattern of people-pleasing behaviour, they often lower their heads physically to demonstrate a submissive state and to show they're not a threat. These slight posture changes are very subtle and many people do it unconsciously, but if you notice you're doing this, or certain people in your team keep doing this, stop and think about why that might be.

There's another model where people move their dominant hand forward into the screen when they gesticulate, forcefully expressing their dominance in a very subtle way. It's necessary to consider what this communicates in a wider context. So next time you're in a meeting, in an online call or just in real life, watch and notice what is happening with the sound turned down. You can learn an awful lot.

Then there is our gut. There's value that comes from what has been described as our 'second brain'. According to research done by Harvard Medical School, your gut and your brain are in constant communication.[36] Byproducts from gut bacteria have been proven to affect how we think, how we behave and our moods. How often have you experienced 'butterflies' in your stomach due to nerves, or nausea before a big presentation? Listen to your gut, physically but also intuitively. It will reveal more than you realise.

Side Note

The human gut is called the enteric nervous system; with more than 500 million nerves, it's the most complex neural network after our brain. It's also unique in that it can operate somewhat independently of the brain and central nervous system. This has led some scientists to refer to it as our 'second brain'.

Life might be a lot easier if we were all machines, and we could put the data in and get the outputs we need.

But we aren't.

We're humans dealing with humans. Try as we might, none of us are 100% rational. Even the senior scientists we work with! Trusting your head, the data and the tangible inputs means we often forget to trust what our gut is telling us. We are creatures of habit, and we like to make sense of the world through patterns and predictable behaviour. So if you get a gut feeling about something, investigate that feeling. Trust it may be a combination of past experiences, knowledge or a mix of several inputs you've had in the past, coming together to tell you something.

---

36 Debra Bradley Ruder, 'The Gut and the Brain', *Harvard Medical School* (Winter 2017). https://hms.harvard.edu/news-events/publications-archive/brain/gut-brain, accessed 24 September 2024.

Seeing

We may spend so much time talking and thinking about what to say next that we don't pay enough attention to our other senses. Modern offices with glass walls give an interesting opportunity to 'see' what is happening in a meeting. Next time you walk past one, take time to notice what you can see and what behaviours and emotions you might be seeing expressed.

Let's imagine being offsite at a team workshop. People are standing around a flip chart. This is a modus operandi for collecting and sharing data but again, as the facilitator or the team leader, try to acknowledge and notice where everyone stands. The risk is people default to the lowest level of energy, which is standing at a comfortable distance out of the way. The more introverted people might stand at the back (it's their safe place), while the extroverts might be having a fabulous party at the front of the room to the exclusion of everybody else. Redress the balance and ask a person at the back to read out one of the points on the board. Ask someone at the front to role-play a scene. Ask everyone to take four steps forward. As the leader or facilitator, it's your responsibility to capture and harness the energy of the room.

In Nancy Kline's book, *Time to Think*, she wrote that 'the quality of a person's attention determines the quality of other people's thinking.'[37] So, if you're with a team or in a meeting and you're there for the purpose and the success of that situation, be 100% present. Put your phone away, stop making lists, stop multitasking, stop trying to do something else. Be fully present. Our full attention is one of the greatest gifts we have to offer a colleague.

---

37 Nancy Kline, *Time to Think: Listening to Ignite the Human Mind* (London: Cassell Illustrated, 2021).

Have you ever heard someone say, 'It's OK, I'm listening …' while they are doing something else?

Are they listening?

It's certainly true that in one-to-one work, you might only have five minutes to speak to a colleague, but make those five minutes count. Put your distractions away and go for a walk together. Concentrate 100% on what you are doing. Use all your senses. Look, listen, notice, feel. Be purposeful and present in all that you do. We need to show up as our whole selves, both our rational and emotional selves, to be an authentic leader that people need.

There are so many external stimuli and competing sources of distraction when we're at work. There's always constant pinging for your attention or someone who needs to talk and with all of these, you know you are needed, you are necessary and you are important. It's a strong dopamine hit.

But it's important not to allow these dopamine hits to distract you and cause your attention to leave the present. Even in a virtual meeting where you think a quick glance at your device won't be harmful – it is. By allowing your attention to break, you signal your attention has left the room and you risk chipping away or losing the energy and connection you have with your colleagues.

And with that goes the trust and relationship you're working so hard to build.

All of this is about recognising the context we are working within and having an awareness of the system: to understand the bigger picture as well as the finer details. Once we understand and recognise what the system needs, the answer then is not to wade in and save the day. Don't assume your role as a leader is to fly in and magically fix everything. Your team might not need or want you to, and leaping into a situation where your presence isn't needed is like diving into a beehive without assessing the *entire* situation first: you could get stung. If a team needs our direct intervention, let's pause and check that is what they need right now before wading in and offering it. (Writing this makes me think of my young children trying to zip up their coats themselves. Don't assume they want us to do it for them!)

So, use all of your senses first.

Assess the situation: what would help right now? Would they like you to listen or to provide advice? Would they like you to ask some questions to deepen their own understanding? Or would they like you to do something else?

More often than not, they will tell you what they need if you ask and give them time and space to think. And whatever their answer is, you do. With 100% commitment.

A good leader will be able to use all of their senses like a superpower to understand what is really happening at a deeper level. So pause before jumping into action. When you do, you give someone the greatest gift you can offer as a leader: your full attention. And no one will get stung!

Response

by Suzanne Lee to
Sensing the System: Avoid Being Stung!

Suzanne is the head of Global Talent, Learning and Organisation Development for a global medical device company. She is committed to continuous learning and is currently completing her PhD in Organisational Change, focusing on the dynamics of intimacy and power within growing organisations.

Why are we trying to avoid the sting? If we try too hard to avoid the sting, then we won't even engage, or step into the water far enough, deep enough to be fully committed, fully into the relationship. We might be holding back and generally the other party will feel it, at some level. Does the relationship stay on only the surface transactional level: actions, outcomes, obstacles? Is it just about getting stuff done?

What are we afraid of with the sting – the pain, the discomfort, the ambiguity of how long it might last and the consequences? This made me reflect on so-called difficult conversations and how many of us sometimes (often?) avoid these at all costs because of the potential sting that might come with them, in the moment or as a longer-term consequence if we don't 'get it right', whatever that means. It might be more helpful to accept we can never get it 'right' because it very much depends on the interactions, the experiences, the emotions and the context at the time. Maybe all we can ever hope for is to live up to our own best intentions. The most impactful leaders are those who will see the best in you and hold you to account to live up to that. This includes hard truths, tough love if you will: constructive feedback as well as appreciation of you as a person and of your strengths. If you know this person has your best interests at heart, then you can trust the intentions are caring and supportive, even if the words aren't perfect, even if it isn't exactly how you might have said it.

One key to improving your relationships and your own self-development over time: being open to and asking regularly for feedback and guidance. Be as specific as possible to help people help you. Rather than a general 'I would love to get some feedback from you' or 'do you have some feedback for me?', how about: 'I am working on presenting with confidence so I would love to get your input and feedback on my presentation this morning, what worked well and what I could do differently in the future.'

Feedback, of course, is a two-way process. What is the only way to respond to feedback? Saying 'Thank you', as it truly is a gift. When you are able to see yourself anew, then you are able to construct a new way of being: to notice when you are being triggered, when you are feeling a strange emotion, and stay with it because it has a message to tell. Self-feedback is also possible. One of the most impactful exercises in self-development is to focus on a topic, such as improving team relationships, then take five or ten minutes per day to journal on your experiences of the day in the context of team relationships. What happened? How did it feel? What did you sense? How might you want to act differently next time? This way you can watch yourself progress over time, day by day, little by little. Consistency of action is the key!

This leads me to the other big topic that for me is so important: the use of those senses, not just to assess the situation outside of self, but first and foremost to assess the situation inside of self. To be in tune with the system is a key strength of leadership and will take you far. However, if you are not in tune with yourself, then it will be more difficult for you to distinguish between your feelings and those of the people in the system. There will be a risk that you project what you are feeling out onto those around you. For example, if you are sensing people are anxious, how will you know if that is your own anxiety being manifested or if it's really something in the system? Where do you stop and where does the system begin? What are the boundaries you need to hold to feel whole, valued and authentic? In times of change and transformation, I suggest that this is the first place to start. As Bill O'Brien, former CEO of Hanover Insurance, said: 'The success of an intervention depends on the interior condition of the intervener.'[38] Otto Scharmer's Theory U approach puts it another way: 'The success of our actions as change-makers does not depend on *what* we do or *how* we do it, but on the *inner place* from which we operate.'[39]

Where to start? Mindfulness and going within: paying attention to your breath, breathing in, breathing out. When your mind starts to wander, perfect: catch it and redirect it back to the breath. Your mind will wander; this is entirely normal, and the aim is not to stop it happening (it would not be possible in any case!). It is the act of catching your mind wandering and redirecting it that builds the mindfulness and inner awareness muscle. Start small; two minutes a day is where I started. Seriously, you can't say you haven't got time for that! The key is to make it consistent and a habit over time, building up to fifteen or so minutes. I highly recommend Dr Amishi Jha's book, *Peak Mind*, as an excellent science-based overview of the latest research and easy-to-try

38 C. Otto Scharmer, *The Essentials of Theory U: Core Principles and Applications*, large print edition (Oakland, CA: Berrett-Koehler Publishers, Inc., 2018), 7.

39 Otto Scharmer and Katrin Kaufer, *Leading from the Emerging Future: From Ego-System to Eco-System Economies* (San Francisco: Berrett-Koehler, 2013), 18.

exercises.[40] She says her research has proven just twelve minutes a day is all you need! It could be the best twelve minutes you ever invest in your own well-being.

---

40 Amishi P. Jha, *Peak Mind* (London: Piatkus, 2021).

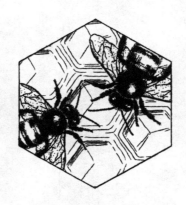

WINTER

Winter brings the natural cycle of life to a close. It is time to repair and protect: time to prepare for the cold harsh weather. Flowering plants and bees focus on self-preservation and protection. Trees lose their leaves and their sap stops flowing. Perennials such as crocus and grape hyacinth conserve energy in their bulbs safe below ground.

In working life, the year's end is also one of closure. It may be a natural deadline for projects to finish, or sales cycles and budgets to be completed. From a human resource perspective this is often when performance is assessed, and goals measured. It is a good time for review, reflection and rest, ready to start the cycle again in spring.

In this section, we look at:

[10]

Endings: Wintering

'Begin at the beginning,' the King said gravely,
'and go on till you come to the end: then stop.'
– LEWIS CARROLL, *Alice's Adventures in Wonderland*, 1865.

In this chapter, we will think about the end of the yearly cycle for bees and
reflect on the importance of successful beginnings, middles and endings at work.

B Y MID-AUGUST IN EUROPE we are approaching the end of the cycle for flowering plants. The majority of them have done their work and been fertilised, and don't need nectar or bright colours to attract hard-working honey bees. They are putting their energy into the generative work of developing fruits.

In the beehive it is the end of the cycle too; the goal has turned from growth and development to one of survival. The queen no longer needs to lay eggs and the bees must prepare for a long, dark winter. This means the male drones face a harsh reality: homicide! They are no longer needed by the hive and are either forcefully ejected, stung to death or, being wholly reliant on the female worker bees and unable to feed themselves, they are left to starve.

The worker bees' sole job now is to keep the queen warm and fed until spring. In Alsace when the first hedgerow blossoms appear, such as the white flowers of blackthorn in early March, it's a telltale sign the seasons have changed and that there are enough food supplies for the queen to start laying her eggs again. Until then, they will be using their precious reserves of honey to sustain her and the rest of the hive.

As the temperature drops at the beginning of winter there may only be about 20,000 bees left to keep the queen warm. To do so, the remaining bees form a ball or a nucleus around the queen and bundle together tightly. Then one bee crawls to the outside of the ball, eats a bellyful of sugar-rich honey, prepared just for this very reason, and crawls back through the tightly formed insulating ball of bees. She will position herself alongside the queen and release heat from her flight muscles by shivering. The worker bee then commits her final act of servitude by crawling back out to the edge of the tight ball of bees – and dying, falling to the floor of the hive.

The inside of a beehive is always kept fastidiously clean, and a small number of bees tasked with this role will eject her body quickly out of the front door to the welcoming birds outside. In fact in winter, if you see a few dead bees or even feeding birds at the entrance of a hive you know all is well inside. But for how much longer, who knows? This carries on all the way until the first hopeful signs of spring when there may only be a few hundred bees left: life hangs in the balance. If March is cold and damp and the pollen and nectar can't be matured, it is even more high risk. Touch and go.

And so the cycle of the bees' annual hard work comes to an end. Ready to start again in spring.

Everything in life is a cycle of beginnings, middles and endings. As humans, we have a unique and dynamic way of interacting with our environment, and it is when this process is interrupted or left unfinished that problems come up. The Gestalt cycle of experience is a central tenet of Gestalt therapy and conceptualises this process as a cycle of sensation, awareness, mobilisation, action, contact, satisfaction and withdrawal as we respond to arising needs. A very simple example of this might be an individual who is studying, when they notice a gnawing feeling in their stomach (sensation). Being a common daily experience they immediately recognise they are hungry (awareness) and start wondering what to eat for lunch (mobilisation). They get up from their desk and head to a local café where they order a sandwich (action). As they bite into the sandwich they experience a delightful pleasure (contact) until they have finished it and no longer feel hungry (satisfaction). At this point, they leave the café to continue studying (withdrawal). This is a whole cycle with a beginning, a middle and an end.

If only all change, and all cycles of experience were that simple. If they were, of course, coaches would be out of a job! As you can see, this cycle can apply to many different situations and experiences.

In Western society, we are more emotionally familiar and linguistically comfortable with the beginning of this cycle, than the end. Therefore, it's easy for us to have a natural bias for the front end of this spectrum. A quick look at my garden reveals how good I am at starting projects but not naturally attentive to finishing things well!

In the work we do with leaders, teams and organisations, we notice how often energy is put into starting a project or a workstream or change initiative. Endings, however, are rarely conducted well. Elements, decisions and conversations are left open, a bit like leaving multiple browser tabs open on your laptop. By the end of the day, your personal operating system is running too hot and too slowly, as you continue to process data for everything simultaneously. No wonder we burn out!

It is difficult to start anything well unless we have the end in mind. But we can't end well unless we have considered the beginning. It's a cycle.

Let's take the example of meetings. They seem to be the key unit of activity at work, yet rarely are they ever run effectively. If they were, the working world would be a better, more efficient place. How often have meetings started well with energy, debate and engagement, only for one person to leave early without announcing, or particularly online, for meetings to end abruptly due to time constraints? Often we end with no clear actions or follow-up. As the screens close mid-sentence on 'I'll email you', we then proceed to the next meeting and the next. By the end of the day, we are left with even more browsers left open on our overworked personal operating system.

At Hive-Logic we apply the same arc of beginning-middle-end to designing, running and facilitating meetings with a conscious attention to closing well, and there are a number of frameworks we apply. One is the GROW model developed by Sir John Whitmore and his peers in the late 1980s.[41]

- **G** stands for Goal and where the client wants to be.
- **R** is for the Reality of the current situation: what are the issues, the baseline, and how far away is the client from their goal?

---

41 John Whitmore, *Coaching for Performance: Growing Human Potential and Purpose*, 4th edition (London: Nicholas Brealey Publishing, 2009).

- **O** is for Obstacles and Options: what are the blocks standing in the client's way and what are their options for solving it?
- And **W** is for the Way Forward: the action steps that need to be taken.

One of the benefits of this framework is that it starts with the end in mind and focuses on a good, clear conclusion. It can also be an effective model to structure meetings and workshops.

Another model that provides a good framework and helps to lead to a good close is the 4C model developed by Dave Kesby. We often use this in meeting planning and design, and it can help ensure enough time is given to consider the real issues, before landing on a good close.

- Connect: let's all check in at a human level. Let's be fully present for the task ahead.
- Consider: what is the topic today, and what do we need to think about?
- Change: what action do we need to take as a result?
- Close: what needs to be said to close well?

Now let's focus on new projects. They are easy to announce and are heralded with a fanfare. We put energy into forming a 'workstream', we have the endorsement of a senior sponsor or board member, and we may recruit a new consulting firm to help. A project may start with much positive energy and have its own identity, even a logo or project name.

However, the end of a project may not always be a success. When it doesn't produce the results heralded at the beginning it can be difficult to know how to respond or how to process it. Failure doesn't seem to be an acceptable outcome, which is just another example of not having the emotional maturity or language to discuss the closing phase of a project.

This is important to acknowledge and to learn from. It's very common to label the start of a project as a 'pilot study': a small-scale phase that has a reduced investment and a reduced risk, but it starts with the expectation that it will be a success and then scaled up.

Instead of 'pilot studies', the London Business School advocates the use of the term 'experiments'. Experiments are designed with a hypothesis that can then be proved or disproved. For a hypothesis to be disproved is not a failure; it is an incremental phase of learning. The results can be considered objectively and then the learnings from the conclusions can be discussed. This reframing can be a very positive approach to closing an exploratory phase of a project well, before starting the new phase from a good position.

In our own Hive-Logic projects, because I know endings are not my natural strength, I ensure we pay attention to a good close to a project by asking for client feedback. When feedback is received we donate to the charity, Bees for Development. This helps me to pay attention to closing well and signals to the client that we have had a clean end. A win-win for everyone, and the bees!

What about changing job roles? It's easy to celebrate starting a new job with a post on LinkedIn. New employees starting at an organisation will be welcomed with bunches of flowers and perhaps a welcome committee. Introductory drinks and lunches are planned, and we might receive good luck cards and gifts. But despite all of that effort to begin well, what happens at the end?

When a new leader (or any employee) starts a new role in a team it is important to start well by ensuring the old chapter has closed. The previous individual may still 'cast a shadow' over the team and people may all be at different stages of grieving (or celebrating!) the end of the previous era.

An important early step is to acknowledge this phase. Celebrate and capture everything that was good about the previous phase and agree to keep those behaviours. But it's also a chance to reflect on what activities and behaviours were not supporting the team and that can be let go.

A simple ceremony, such as a glass of prosecco and a toast to be grateful for the past and to let it go, can help to mark this transition. A team photo is another important ceremony that can signal this closing of an old team and the start of a new one. This is an important process for everyone to let go of the old and close well, before starting on the best foot. A team can now focus all their energy on a new beginning, to 'press reset' if necessary.

A person moving to another role in an organisation is often pressured to start the new one quickly and not finish the old one well. Who has ever had a really thorough handover from the departing manager? Who has ever been able to close all the elements and share the learning and wisdom accrued?

One organisation we work with, Branding Science, solved this by championing short videos to be made by the stakeholders. The goal is to capture the biggest learnings in a quick and effective format, so this knowledge would be retained and not lost when a leader quickly moves in to a new role.

Organisational wisdom and value have the potential to get lost and we need to pay more attention to how they are shared. Take a moment to think about your handover processes and what you can do to make the departing and incoming individuals get what they need in the transition. We need to close well, before we can begin the next step in the cycle well.

Coming to the end of a job has the same inevitability as starting one, and we may finish jobs for many reasons – with some reasons easier to acknowledge than others.

We note there are three distinct points of leaving: to leave with one's head, one's heart and one's body. In my own experience of leaving a large company after nearly two decades, my head had already left and I was looking forward to taking my new steps. I had the energy for a new beginning.

My body, however, was still turning up and doing the work, and that brought its own physical and emotional challenges. It only truly left on the official deadline.

I did feel that my heart, or part of it, was still strongly connected to the organisation after such a large part of my working life and it took me some months after officially leaving the organisation to finally feel emotionally free and disconnected.

At that point, I felt I had closure with my head, my body and my heart and I could wholly align myself with my new company. These three important steps rarely seem to happen at the same point, but closure or a good ending can't happen until the three steps have taken place.

In meetings and in life, everything comes to an end. It's easy to celebrate new life, birth announcements and celebrations. That comes easily, but it should be no surprise that some decades later life also comes to an end.

In Western society, we seem less emotionally competent to deal with it. We can be left not knowing what to say or avoiding the topic entirely. However, as with everything in life, learning how to handle endings with sensitivity and awareness is a skill and it can be learned. If you feel you do not have the experience or skills to address conflicts and difficult issues, especially in relation to endings, seek out mentors or a coach and opportunities that can help you improve. Endings are difficult for obvious reasons but that is not an excuse to avoid developing the maturity and knowledge about how one must deal with them. We should all lean into endings with curiosity and care, and acknowledge that while they are difficult, they are inevitable and just one step in a huge ongoing cycle of beginnings, middles and endings.

So, like the bees (but preferably without the homicide), pay more attention to closing one phase well before you can have a good start to the next one.

Response

by John Leary-Joyce to
Endings: Wintering

John is the author of The Fertile Void: Gestalt Coaching at Work *and* Systemic Team Coaching. *He was co-founder of the Gestalt Centre London in 1979 and founder of the Academy of Executive Coaching, AoEC.com, in 1999. He combines his individual/team coaching, supervision and training with a passion for dancing Argentine tango – always in the moment.*

As a Gestalt coach, trainer and supervisor with individuals and teams, I was really inspired to expand on Philip's beginnings and endings, drawing further parallels with the hive at this phase of its life.

Managing endings well is such a challenge, as Philip explains. Our bees don't have expectations on how it should be; they know their role and simply do their job in service of the system until they're finished. They don't need a GROW model since they don't need goals, but in our human systems, we have to manufacture that collaboration, trust and unified direction – a job for leaders and coaches.

Bees know instinctively the priorities of their system, building resources during the season of growth for use in this season of scarcity. They are totally present in the moment, and don't have a selfish greed to be individually wealthy and become successful in the future.

As Philip outlines, the GROW model helps us humans first identify our future aspirations and goals, then attend to the reality of the current context. At this phase of the lifecycle, that may mean accepting the reality as it is and letting go of what has not been achieved. Too often, individuals and teams want to deny the difficulties of perceived 'failures'. Our job as leaders/coaches is to gently but firmly guide the team to 'face the brutal facts', often facing strong (usually suppressed) emotions of anger or grief. Unlike our bees, who aren't troubled by emotions (as far as we know), a key part of our existence is managing the complexity of relationships.

When we're in harmony and 'flow', like the bees, then the Gestalt cycle is simply how we work and live. Like them, we're also hardwired to complete each action/interaction – the meaning of Gestalt, but unlike the bees we interrupt the natural flow, generating blocks to that energy and excitement, which then creates anxiety and fear. Our job as leaders/ coaches is often to slow down the impulse to rush into action and take time in the sensation/awareness stage of the cycle to pay attention to unpleasant emotions, especially if they carry the fear of failure.

This is where Gestalt aligns with the London Business School view of treating new ventures (or coaching interventions) as experiments – testing a sound hypothesis to see if it works and remembering to 'lean into endings with curiosity and care'.

Our body is the reservoir of emotions, as Philip outlines in his lovely example of leaving his organisation first with his head, then body and finally heart. Too often, our head overrules our heart and body, which in the extreme leads to burnout: a major reason for coming to coaching or therapy. Our bees don't have this problem; they do what's needed without emotion and simply end their lives in service of the community.

One final comment relating to the W of GROW. As Philip does, this is usually described as 'Way Forward' but originally John Whitmore had the W as 'Will' – focusing more on the energy and determination to undertake the task ahead rather than the task itself. This attention to the process rather than outcomes fits closer with the Gestalt view on emergent outcomes and somewhat closer to the bees' perspective.

So to end the gestalt of this commentary, I'm reflecting on how we – personally and with our teams/clients – achieve the balance between self and community service, and between the importance of managing endings with satisfaction and closure.

11

New Beginnings: Preparing the Hive

Isn't it funny
How a bear likes honey?
Buzz, buzz, buzz,
I wonder why he does?

– A. A. MILNE, *Winnie-the-Pooh*, 1926.

As the bees are focused on keeping the queen warm and nourished, the beekeeper can turn his attention to closing the year well for himself too. In this chapter, we will review and reflect on what has worked well, and what hasn't over the past year: relevant for beekeeping and the bigger picture aspects of our work and life.

WINTER IS A GOOD TIME to prepare our hives and tools ready for the spring. The wooden boxes that were so heavy when full of frames of honey now need to be cleaned, sanded and painted. Inside, the boxes are coated with propolis (or bee glue, as it's commonly called). It's a resinous mixture that honey bees produce by mixing saliva and beeswax with sticky sap gathered from tree buds.

Bees use it as a sealant for unwanted open spaces in the beehive; it keeps out draughts and holds the parts of the beehive closely together. It also darkens the inside of the hive, which the bees prefer to new wood. However, it also sets as strongly as glue so you will need to use a blowtorch to melt this off and scrape it away. It's great fun, but be careful not to set fire to your equipment. (There's always a lot to think about and many things that can go wrong for the enthusiastic beekeeper!)

Tools need to be cleaned and sharpened. It's also time to pay attention to your gloves, bee-proof suit and veil. Often they need repairing as they get holes in them, so gaffer tape is an essential part of a beekeeper's armamentarium. After all, there's nothing between the end of your nose and an anxious bee once it's trapped inside the protective veil of your bee suit.

One of my favourite closing tasks at this time of year is recycling old beeswax comb. This comes from old, damaged frames or the wax left over when scraping the wax caps off the cells after harvesting honey. We leave the combs outside where the bees can eat the remaining sticky honey, leaving the old beeswax behind. That wax can then be melted gently in an old saucepan to make candles, ready for Christmas and the dark nights of winter. The smell from the beeswax candles is divine: another source of sweetness and light.

All of these practical steps are a good closure of the previous year and a good investment for the year ahead. The most important step, though, is more cerebral than hands-on, and that is to reflect and review how the year has gone. More importantly, to note what we have learnt about the bees and about ourselves as beekeepers. I like to keep a plastic wallet of notes tucked under the roof of each hive because at a practical level, they all begin to look the same after a while.

This end-of-year reflection is something we can apply to our work life. It's not about reflecting on our purpose or our place in life, rather this is a more deliberate reflection on the year just passed and the year ahead, as the world slows down for the end-of-year celebrations.

How did our working year go?

What could be improved for next year?

What do we need to pay more attention to?

As the beekeeper checks his tools, it's a good reminder for us all to be on top of our game and ensure our axe is sharp before the next season. From the physical tools and machinery you use to keep your business running to your own personal box of skills, what needs to be repainted or mended? What needs to be replaced or upgraded?

Don't assume that just because you've gotten this far and you're in this role that it will continue unchallenged, or that things won't break down or malfunction – literally or metaphorically.

I've seen it before: an arrogance in those who believe they've gotten so far in their career they don't need to invest in themselves anymore. But the status that comes with a senior role can very easily be taken away and you risk being left with nothing. The world is changing pretty quickly, and in the knowledge economy we are in today, you can be out of date before you realise it. Other colleagues, and hiring managers, may already realise it before you do!

The risk of not evolving is that you suddenly find yourself without a relevant and valuable set of skills at the age of forty, fifty or fifty-five. That can be a very threatening proposition. Fear can set in, which can lead to unconstructive behaviours and defensiveness. We often see people hanging on in a job they're not happy with because they are not willing to let go of a role or do the work necessary to improve. When an organisation or leader is unable to evolve and change, it manifests in poor leadership, unhappiness, cynicism and overwhelm. People burn out and organisations begin to struggle.

It's more of a risk *not* to evolve.

Just because you've done well so far, come from a certain background, have certain connections, and have followed a particular path doesn't grant you anything. That's not a complaint or a warning, but rather a sign to keep evolving and adapting to what the world wants and needs. While being a leader who falls into a certain category might have been a great advantage in the past for many reasons, it's not a guarantee for the future.

To avoid that happening, you need to acknowledge the changes that will appear in the coming year, be aware of the potential impact and embrace it.

One example of changes to prepare for is Artificial Intelligence, or AI. At the time of writing this book, AI has begun to make its mark in the workplace as well as changing attitudes to remote working. New roles such as 'prompt engineers' for AI, 'fractional COOs' and 'digital health coaches' have appeared. Karim Lakhani, a professor at Harvard Business School and author of *The Age of AI*, wrote an article called 'AI won't replace humans – but humans with AI will replace humans without AI', and I think that's very poignant.[42] Leaders must be open to change, and allow space and time for experimentation so we can continue to be flexible in the knowledge economy. Change has become a constant, and change management will become one of the most important skills in your toolbox. It's your responsibility to ensure that particular axe is

---

42   Karim R Lakhani, 'AI Won't Replace Humans – But Humans With AI Will Replace Humans Without AI', *Harvard Business Review* (4 August 2023). https://hbr.org/2023/08/ai-wont-replace-humans-but-humans-with-ai-will-replace-humans-without-ai, accessed 24 September 2024.

especially sharp. Develop into someone who embraces and is curious about change, rather than one who fears and tries to prevent it. You don't want to become a leader who is replaced by another – one better equipped to handle change.

For the Hive-Logic team, it's been a real joy to adopt technology for virtual meetings, and we have enjoyed integrating Miro and Mural into our processes. Both are digital platforms that empower teams to collaborate remotely and while initially hesitant about whether or not individuals would benefit from it, we've been happy with the results.

SpatialChat was used to great effect in the 2021 Teal Around the World conference. We had hundreds of people online, using different online chat rooms and virtual bars as digital spaces to connect in small groups. Meaningful conversations were had, and new connections were made.

I remember at one point, I needed a break and moved to a quiet corner of a virtual room for a moment of introverted recharge while I observed multiple small group conversations happening across the room. Art and science imitating life! We have also been using SessionLab, Asana and Slack to collaborate and design meetings and are using AI programs to write transcripts and summaries of meetings and interviews. These all allow us more time to think about the meaning and depth of our work.

Let's also take time to apply our best strategic thinking to ourselves. We all like to talk about strategy – our five-year goals and one-year plans for work – but I rarely see that being applied to our lives away from the office. While taking time to pause and reflect on the year's end, it's important to acknowledge key elements outside of work.

As a family unit, how are we doing? What do we need more of?

What do our children need from us right now, and what will they need in the coming months?

What will our parents or extended family need from us next year?

How are my social connections, and are there any I need to work on?

How good are my professional connections outside my current employer?

Do I need to invest more in my health?

What do I need to be doing differently by this time next year?

And then connected to that, a good, sensible question about finance. What state are our finances in and what else do we need to consider? If you have almost paid your mortgage off and your kids are leaving for university, the coming year might be the right time to think about change. If you are lucky enough not to need to keep earning at the same level, do you need to keep doing it? And why?

All of these points make for a useful personal end-of-year review and a good stepping stone towards considering our purpose: something we will explore in the next chapter. For your personal end-of-year review, I would like you to consider these three simple questions:

1. What do I need more of?
2. What do I need to stop doing?
3. What else do I need to consider?

Take time for personal reflection, and to discuss as a family. These closing reflections are an essential part of life's cycle that are very easy to avoid or to skip over. Such questions may be simple but the answers might be difficult. Or revealing. Or liberating. If you need to, reach out to a trusted thinking partner or coach to help you with process and accountability. If we are to continually learn and grow and make a valuable contribution to our sphere of work, and the world around us, we must make time to consider this.

So stop.

Pause.

And take time to think.

Response

by Guy Dickinson to
New Beginnings: Preparing the Hive

Guy is a behavioural scientist and has a long career in Pharma and consulting to support behavioural change, capability building, strategy and innovation. He has a specific interest in digital transformation, AI and the future of work. He was most recently head of Employee Experience at Novartis.

Reading Philip's description of seasonal rituals made me wonder why it feels so much harder to approach questions of repair, recombination and removal in our work. I'd like to share some questions and concepts that this chapter prompted me to think about.

Seasons and Anchors

I realised that while I adore the renewal of colour and texture a change of season brings, equivalent symbols of transition are rather absent in my virtual, hybrid, digital work environments. In contrast to beekeeping, the artefacts of our work vanish with the close of a laptop lid, and our software 'tools' maintain themselves silently in the background. Our work environments lack signs of change and progress that prompt reflection and renewal.

When we eventually make changes in our work (or events force us to), I've noticed a tendency to add 'things' to our role, responsibilities and organisation, rather than work at repair, replacement or removal.

Is this perhaps a consequence of losing those physical signs of renewal? Does their absence lead us to default to a more reactive, familiar urge to add and hoard? There is comfort in holding onto things, including projects, titles and status. There can be fear in letting go. Do we lack the beekeeper's ability to think about our workplace 'tools' with the same intent of repair, recombination and removal that Philip applies during his seasonal maintenance rituals?

Sticky Questions

Philip mentioned how AI is impacting his work, and I wanted to talk about AI too. I think it is a 'forcing' moment that is an opportunity to ask about where AI might help us repair, recombine, or even remove things in our work.

- How will our work change as a result?
- What do we need to focus on most?
- Where should we be focusing our energy?
- How will our teams change as a result?
- As a leader, what questions should I be asking and helping my organisation answer?

I've found that when I raise these points – of myself, peers, and an organisation – we soon end up in a honeycomb of sticky questions that challenge personal and organisational purpose and capabilities.

And so I needed a simple way to understand how work becomes complicated and 'sticky'. What I have found helpful is appreciating and asking how work and the things that support work get *bundled*.

Bundles? Beloved of many internet-era business model discussions, it's one of the most simple and effective ways I've found to explore the complexity of how and why an organisation works.

One example is organisational capability. I'm often asked what capability actually *means*, and how it differs from skills or knowledge. The best explanation I've found is that capability is a bundle. A bundle of:

- Knowledge (knowing *what* it is).
- Skills (knowing *how* to do it).
- Experience (knowing *why* we do it).
- The enablers an organisation provides (technology, resources, etc. to apply it).

My job is a 'bundle' of my capabilities and other organisational resources that I combine in particular (sometimes peculiar) ways to deliver value. My organisation is another bundle; jobs are bundled with workflows, policies, resources and incentives into teams, and teams into departments, and so on. Zoom in (or out) and you see bundles everywhere – individual capabilities, roles, teams, companies, business models, whole industries, even beehives: they're all bundles. And I've found bundles are an effective analogy that help leaders to ask perhaps the most sticky AI question of all: what work can be *unbundled* – and how?

Bundles let us explore these fundamental questions by asking:

- What could we combine differently?
- Who else could tackle parts of this capability bundle?
- What new enablers could we add?
- What could my organisation unbundle?

Looking at our work systems and our lives in this way allows us to be curious about what is needed most and what is most important. With an enquiring mind, AI can be used to help and challenge our thinking.

Layers of Time

Philip's beekeeping analogies are a wonderful addition to the analogies tackling systems and complexity, and the seasonal rituals that trigger his reflection and renewal really stuck with me. The way Philip described the importance of seasons to beekeeping made me think of 'pace layers'. Pace layering is a framework that acknowledges different parts of a system will change at different rates. This can help us to better understand how societies, perhaps the most complex of human systems, evolve through interdependence and change: from core, slow moving layers of 'culture' to the more rapidly changing layers in society, like 'fashion'.

In terms of change management, elements can only change according to their natural rhythm or pace. Each layer must respect the different pace of the others. If commerce, for example, is allowed by governance and culture to push nature at a commercial pace, then all-supporting natural forests, fisheries and aquifers will be lost. If governance is changed suddenly instead of gradually, you get the catastrophic French and Russian revolutions. In the Soviet Union, governance tried to ignore the constraints of culture and nature, while forcing a five-year-plan infrastructure pace on commerce and art. By cutting itself off from both support and innovation, it was doomed.

This framework can be applied to many systems. Frank Duffy, the English architect wrote: 'A building properly conceived has several layers of longevity of built components.'[43] He identified four layers in commercial buildings:

---

43 Stewart Brand, *How Buildings Learn: What Happens After They're Built* (New York: Penguin Books, 1995), 12.

- Shell (lasts maybe fifty years).
- Services (swapped out every fifteen years or so).
- Scenery (interior walls, etc. move every five to seven years).
- Set (furniture, moving sometimes monthly).

This concept can also be applied to the pace of change and need for renewal in our personal lives. Which of our beliefs, values and behaviours need to evolve over what time frame and what needs to remain constant?

We can focus on short-term development needs as well as be aware of longer-term growth needs at the same time. We may focus on a next project or job and the short-term skills needed while also being more aware of a longer-term strategic approach to our whole career and how we add value.

This made me think about how technical skills we use daily could unbundle rapidly with new technologies (like AI), while our core problem-solving abilities or leadership philosophy evolve more slowly and build longer-term value over time.

Understanding pace layers can help us and our organisations approach career development strategically, focusing on both short-term skill acquisition and how this bundles with long-term capability building.

Stewart Brand, author of *The Clock of the Long Now: Time and Responsibility,* collaborated with musician Brian Eno to illustrate pace layers with this image[44]:

44 Stewart Brand, *The Clock of the Long Now: Time and Responsibility* (New York: Basic Books, 1999), 37.

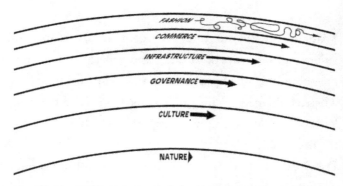

The order of a healthy civilization. The fast layers innovate; the slow layers stabilize.
The whole combines learning with continuity.

You can also think of professional development in terms of pace layers. Ambitious staff will want to know where they are, where they can get to and how to get there. They'll need a framework that provides a clear understanding of what's necessary to advance along a particular track. For such a framework to be successful, it must focus on the things that change at the same speed as a career, and consider them in the context of the needs of an organisation.

Richard Rutter, from design consultancy Clearleft, built on Brand's model to illustrate pace layers in an organisation.[45]

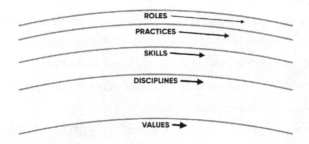

The five levels of pace in the changing requirements of a profession.

45 Richard Rutter, 'Applying Pace Layers to Career Paths', Clearleft blog (28 February 2022). https://clearleft.com/thinking/applying-pace-layers-to-career-paths, accessed 24 September 2024.

From slow to fast:

1. **Values** represent the culture of a company. A meaningful set of values leads to ways of working and general competencies that are shared by all employees, but that will vary little over time. These could include core skill sets such as communication, problem solving, leadership and empathy, which are shared across the organisation.

2. **Disciplines** are the different groups of skills an organisation needs to function. They will only change when the organisation fundamentally changes the services or products it provides. Examples of these groups of skills are operations, finance, design, strategy, marketing, development. You should not think of them as teams or departments, but skill sets used in differing proportion by people across the organisation. A marketer, for example, will lean heavily on specialised marketing skills but may also be required to perform some aspects of design, strategy and finance.

3. **Skills** are the outcomes the disciplines are there to achieve. Core *communication* skills might include collaboration, presentation and feedback. Design-specific skills could include exploration, production craft and validation.

4. **Practices** are how you do your job on a day-to-day basis – the tools, techniques and activities used. These can be quite fluid and change quickly – at the speed of fashion, to use Brand's metaphor – but the outcomes they achieve will remain largely unchanged in the short term.

5. **Job roles** – the actual jobs or job titles people have – can change quickly but the underlying skills required across the board remain the same. For example, an organisation might decide to swap out its generalists in favour of specialists, but while the job roles

have changed, the practices and skills remain largely untouched, albeit they will be combined in different ways.

Of these layers, it is the values, disciplines and skills that move at the speed of a career. Applied to professional development it is therefore the combination of skills, and competency required of them, which should form a framework to help people judge where they are in their career, and where they should or could get to.

What does this mean for you and your career?

What are you curious about and what is it making you think?

12

Purpose: Sweet Honey

You find peace not by rearranging the circumstances of your life,
but by realizing who you are at the deepest level.
– Eckhart Tolle, *Stillness Speaks*, 2003.

Bees have a single-minded purpose and that is to support the genetic survival
and longevity of the hive. Part of that mission involves making honey. In this
final chapter, we will reflect on the importance of finding our purpose and how
we can do so through self-reflection and exploration.

THROUGHOUT HISTORY, honey has been worshipped and revered as food for the gods, and rightly so. Some consider it a superfood. It contains pinocembrin, which is effective at improving the function of the human brain. It's also antibiotic, antipyretic, antiseptic and antioxidant. It has been used to treat wounds and can contribute to the improvement of gastrointestinal and neurological issues. We know that honey has a shelf life of over four and a half thousand years, as it was found fresh enough to eat in the Egyptian pharaohs' tombs in Giza.

What's not to love about honey?

We all have emotional connections to eating honey, too, from sooth-ing us in a hot drink with lemon when we're ill with a winter cold, to enjoying it drizzled on dessert. I remember opening a jar of my dear Uncle Jack's honey and having it on hot toast after coming home from school. What a lovely, sweet and sticky treat. My favourite type of honey is a wonderful, clear, runny honey made from the flowers of acacia trees pollinated after midsummer. Many of our dear colleagues, friends and clients have tasted our own Hive-Logic honey, and it really does have a particular flavour dependent on the timing of the harvest and the specific location where it was produced in Alsace.

The taste of honey varies throughout the seasons, depending on the flowers that have been pollinated. The first honey to be produced comes from the white buckthorn in the hedgerows, then apple trees with their characteristic white blossoms, then the vibrant pink cherry orchards, followed by wild meadow flowers. These are followed by the rich sources from lime trees and acacia in July. In August, a beekeeper may move his bees closer to a lavender crop, and the bees will swarm and buzz and feast and thrive entirely on the lavender for a couple of weeks. From that, you get the distinctive darker honey with a hint of lavender.

In late September and October, the bees can take sweet sugary sap from pine trees. Helpful aphids bite through the thick pine needles to lap up their own food needs, and the saccharine liquid seeps out of the holes left behind. (You may have noticed this if you have ever parked your car under a pine tree and returned to find a sticky sap over the roof.) The bees can harvest this sugar syrup to create a beautiful dark-coloured and richly-flavoured pine tree honey. This is a beautiful product and distinctly different in flavour from honey made from flower nectar.

After October, if the weather is warm enough for the bees to fly, the lone ivy bush provides a sparse but important source of food through to Christmas.

Let's be thankful to the bees and their single-minded purpose. As we marvel and think about what the bees do, let's apply that same question to ourselves.

What is our purpose in our short time on Earth?

And what will be *our* sweet contribution to the world?

Defining our purpose is a fundamentally difficult process, and in the busyness of our daily life, like the bees, it's easy never to stop and consider this. But what is it? Anita Rolls, founder of the Career Intelligence Academy,[46] defines it as our unique contribution to the world, or UCW. What is the value we contribute to the world?

One way we can explore this is to follow Clayton Christensen's approach. As a professor at Harvard Business School, he taught aspiring MBA students how to apply management and innovation theories to build stronger companies. But he also believed these business models and ways of thinking should be applied to help us lead better lives. It's not just an MBA lesson in running a business. It's about running 'You Inc'.

His best-selling book, *How Will You Measure Your Life?*, opens up these questions and suggests not to save your best strategic thinking for work but to apply it to your family life and everything around you as well. [47] This is something I mentioned in the last chapter as an application to use on your personal end-of-year review. But for this chapter, let's widen our thinking and apply it to our purpose.

So, as well as asking, 'How can I be happy in my career over the

---

46 Rolls A. https://careerintelligenceacademy.com.

47 Clayton M. Christensen, James Allworth, and Karen Dillon, *How Will You Measure Your Life?* (London: HarperCollins, 2012).

next five to ten years?' you could also ask, 'How can I be sure that my relationship with my family is an enduring source of happiness? How can I live my life with integrity?'

Let's come back to this daunting question.

Let's actually stop …

Pause …

… and think about it …

… allow your thoughts to drift up to the highest altitude, way above where the bees are buzzing, all the way to the clouds …

What is most important to you?

What do you most want to do with your time and talents?

What do you want to change or bring about in the world?

Don't focus on the obstacles right now or reasons why your purpose might not be practical, or even possible. You can focus on the obstacles later. Just give yourself permission to dream as expansively as possible.

Many of us were taught from a young age that working hard in a good job, paying your mortgage and supporting your family was enough. But none of us were taught to envision and then step into the life we deserve. So, perhaps it's time to unlearn our old teaching. We have every right to find and live the life we choose. No one has permission to limit us. We're all alive on this earth, and busy like the bees, and that's the only qualification we need. But is it really possible to find something according to your purpose, your values and your beliefs?

We work with many senior leaders who are made redundant at a certain age and when they're looking for their next job, they may assume they want the same salary, the same bonus and the same perks. It may seem it is *quantity* that matters, and it's easy not to take time to pause and consider whether any of this is in line with their purpose or values. It's far easier to just benchmark against our peers and assume a bigger salary and bigger visible perks like a British Airways Gold card are enough.

But rather than jumping to the next big corporate career role (that might not happen for everyone), I like to challenge and unpick that belief.

In coaching senior leaders, the first topic people often bring up is: 'Shall I take this job or that job?' But that's a short-term tactical question. Maybe the more important question is: 'Where do you want to be in the next five years and does the next job take you towards where you need to be?' When we're clear about our purpose and what is going to be fulfilling and satisfying, it becomes far easier to make a short-term decision about the next role.

We all have our own attitudes to money and different financial needs, but we should not assume work happiness will be related to absolute salary. Frederick Herzberg, an influential psychologist in business management, asserts that we all want to be valued; we all want those feelings of satisfaction and fulfilment as they contribute to our feelings of recognition.[48] But it's not the size of our salary that will connect us to feelings of recognition; rather, it's our ability to grow in responsibilities, to contribute and to learn. That's why management and leadership, if practised well, can be the noblest of occupations.

I coached one client who had always wanted to be a part-time professor at university. He loves teaching and has a lot of wisdom to share but he just assumed he couldn't make it pay. After taking the practical steps of assessing his true financial status, he realised he could make it work. Now he works part-time as a chief financial officer of a smaller company and teaches two and a half days a week. And he loves it. He's got more energy in his career now than he had in the last twenty years. It's balanced, it pays and it's fulfilling. The bonus is, it's also fun and it's probably going to lead to more of this type of work in the future, which in turn is helping him. He's never been happier. One of his blockers was believing he needed the next job to be of a similar salary, which became a self-limiting belief.

Lynda Gratton wrote a fabulous book called *The 100-Year Life* and in it, she challenges the original assumption that our lives can be neatly packaged into three phases: the first being learning and education, the second being progression through our careers and the third as retirement.[49]

Gratton argues that this three-phase model is no longer relevant and instead, we should embrace multiple phases with constant evolution together with ongoing learning and transformation. Like the

48 Frederick Herzberg, Bernard Mausner, and Barbara Bloch Snyderman, *The Motivation to Work* (New Brunswick, NJ: Transaction Publishers, 2017).

49 Lynda Gratton and Andrew Scott, *The 100-Year Life: Living and Working in an Age of Longevity* (London: Bloomsbury Information, 2016).

bees whose honey evolves and changes with the seasons, why can't our purpose evolve too?

Let's redesign the third phase of our life and career into something different to what's been done before. The idea of viewing our lives and careers in phases can be quite a helpful way to recognise that when we are in these different places in our lives, we can, and perhaps should, try different things. Phase three of your life doesn't have to be retirement if that's not what drives you. You could give back to the community instead, you could return to education, you could become a mentor or advisor – it's up to you.

Not long ago, I found myself in a role that was no longer satisfying, and it took the process of studying, coaching and asking these difficult questions to unpick the beliefs that were blocking my progression. I acknowledged I'd reached phase two of my career, and it was up to me to design what I wanted phase three to be. But it wasn't easy; it was absolutely terrifying. I believed I was entirely financially dependent on one organisation and the very thought of leaving filled me with fear.

However, through having a good coach and through discussing these questions, I was able to put the financial question into perspective and separate fact from emotion. I needed to be aware of the powerful emotions at play before I could address the rational components, just like developing a good business strategy: what are the different strategic options to deliver that salary I need? And then above and beyond that: what do I love to do?

I realised what I needed and wanted to do, and with that learning, I closed phase two and entered phase three, which for me was creating Hive-Logic.

Finding our purpose is not about chasing the next job title or status that we can report on LinkedIn. Work doesn't exist in isolation. It's important to look at the balance not just within our career, but from the perspective of our whole life. It's a more philosophical approach to our relationship with the world and the people around us.

One client we worked with reached a very senior point in his career but was burnt out – and made redundant at the same time. They'd lost their role and with that, all the signs of success and status: their parking place, their corner office, their Gold travel card. As a result, they felt like they'd lost everything. They'd spent the last twenty years being defined by their professional status in society, but now that was taken away, they didn't know who they were.

However, throughout that time, this leader had gained a great many valuable skills. He had enough money to retire, he had cleared the mortgage, and his children had left education. He was able to reframe his situation and realise he didn't want, or need, another big job. What he loved doing was helping young leaders to grow.

He started to work with a startup incubator, coaching young companies and young leaders. He was invited to take some non-executive director board leadership positions and got the opportunity to invest in the organisations and receive stock options.

Soon he was able to let go of the heavy mantle of having status with a big company and was liberated to add value to the whole community, thereby making a successful transition into phase three of his career.

So here's my question to you: if you had only 4,000 weeks to live, how would you spend them? This is a question posed in Oliver Burkeman's book, *Four Thousand Weeks: Time Management for Mortals*, where he explores the concept of limited time. 4,000 weeks is approximately 76.6 years, so when you put it like this, it changes your perspective.[50]

What do you want to do with your 4,000 weeks?

I'm fifty-three and realise I may only have 1,200 weeks left to live. 1,200 Mondays!

This work will take courage. You might realise you're not in the best place or on the right path. Many people reach a senior level in an organisation and all of a sudden wake up and realise either they're not well or they're not happy – or both. (There are many studies linking a sense of purpose to better physical and mental health; your well-being will say a lot about your purpose.) Most of us don't generally do this self-analysis, and it often takes a thinking partner to create a safe space to ask these questions. As coaches, we can help create a very intimate and supportive space to have these difficult discussions because after so long without any thought applied to it, it can be a difficult process to take on alone. Remember: your career never exists in isolation. It's always part of a bigger picture and it affects your whole life. But, as with most leaders and people we work with, there's a risk we are so busy being busy that we don't get a chance to stop and admire the view, to note where we are in life or where we are going.

For those readers of a certain age, there's a very relevant Ferris Bueller quote: 'Life moves pretty fast. If you don't stop and look around once in a while, you could miss it.'[51]

So think of the bees and their greater purpose.

God save the Queen!

---

50 Oliver Burkeman, *Four Thousand Weeks: Time Management for Mortals* (New York: Farrar, Straus and Giroux, 2021).

51 *Ferris Bueller's Day Off* [movie], dir. John Hughes, Paramount Pictures (USA, 1986).

Response

by Jan Liska to
Purpose: Sweet Honey

Jan has been creating products, brands and services setting new standards for beauty, well-being, health and care at L'Oréal, Shiseido and Sanofi. As global innovator, strategist, behaviour researcher and executive coach, Jan opens new possibilities for people to live the best version of their lives, with self-confidence, curiosity and joy.

I believe the optimal way to close this book is to leave you with an invitation, and options, to define, explore and find the purpose that can be truly yours.

If you happen to be in that third phase of life that Philip mentions, where you've had a satisfactory professional career and are in search of new meaning, it may almost be your duty to explore and accomplish your purpose: you are at the peak of your experiences, capacities and strengths, and you are healthy, physically and mentally. In a certain way, you may even see it as a privilege to find yourself at this stage of life when you have the time, experience and ability to find your purpose.

For many people that will not be the case. They do not have the privilege of health or security. It may not be the optimal moment right now because they have been burnt out by a hated job and toxic management – they need to recover. Their loved ones might be sick, and they need to take care of them. So, to these people, I want to say that it's fine to wait to find your purpose. There is no perfect time to start, just the moment you choose to initiate your purpose journey.

Like Philip, I'm an executive coach and I see many clients who could be called 'The Perfectionists of Purpose'. They want to do well since they are used to doing well, and want to do even better now. They fear missing out on finding their purpose, which is impactful for the world, or getting their purpose 'wrong'. I believe this big idea of purpose can be overwhelming because most accomplishments and almost every achievement we see or hear about these days are immense, and amplified by social media. Award-winning teenage actors or singers, kids creating haute couture worn by stars, politicians or activists who are half or even a third of your age. Suddenly, the more ordinary, quiet and invisible life becomes something that is not worth anyone's attention or not meaningful enough.

Yet a purpose doesn't need to be big and vocal – it can be very small if you wish, and very personal. Stop being that perfectionist and start being an explorer of the purpose you wish to own; find one that is entirely yours. It really is variable, and it doesn't have to be about work. It's alright to define your purpose according to exactly what you need at any given moment, and if it's simply to make enough money to feel secure, or care for your family, that's an important purpose too.

What are you ready for in terms of your purpose? The notion of 'readiness' needs to be considered from several perspectives. What I mean by this, is that sometimes your mind feels ready but, perhaps, not your heart or body. Or you might feel the urgency to search for purpose in your heart but your mind is saying, 'Can I do this?' Or it might be busy with other things. Or your body is too exhausted to follow the motivations of your mind and heart.

Being ready and *feeling* ready are not the same, and you don't need to wait. The optimal way to de-risk your journey into finding your purpose is to start experimenting with very small steps. That's the key to discovering what works best for you. Just try one small step, and pivot if needed.

Margaret J. Wheatley has worked with many organisations and communities on organisational issues. In her book, *Restoring Sanity*, she observes we are living in a declining civilisation.[52] In a world getting increasingly complicated and unpredictable, she calls for people who have wisdom, power of impact and generosity to become 'islands of sanity' for others. I'm very inspired by this perspective as it invites us to consider purpose – which we often see as highly intimate – as altruistic. Sometimes becoming an island of sanity for others and creating a safe space is a great purpose. Purpose does not have to be an action; it can be a meaningful presence in someone's life. It can be time you offer to people just to make them feel a specific way, or think a different way. Contributing to someone's life and amplifying someone's purpose this way represents a great purpose. If your superpower, as a leader, is the ability to create an environment that offers others a moment of clairvoyance and discernment so they can change the world, you will have an incredible impact.

Your purpose will produce a moment for someone else to drive a tremendous change. When you're ready, give it a try and apply this purposeful thinking to your teams and your colleagues. And again, you don't have to change your whole company, the whole industry or the world. Just take a first step to create space and time for someone else, so they can be at their best. If you can create something meaningful, at least for one other person than yourself, that's invaluable. Pay attention to

---

52 Margaret J Wheatley, *Restoring Sanity: Practices to Awaken Generosity Creativity, and Kindness in Ourselves and Our Organizations* (Oakland, CA: Berrett-Koehler Publishers, Inc., 2024).

how you feel. If that moment brings you joy, inspiration and satisfaction, it may well be close to your purpose. Give yourself permission to find your purpose in the way you want, at your pace. Don't be judgemental or prescriptive: the decision to find a purpose is yours. It's an invitation to explore. It may also be fine if you don't want to find your purpose right now. It may be that your purpose right now is about enjoying a good life surrounded by your loved ones and that's enough. Maybe you already live your purpose, without having taken the time to frame it with words. Keep exploring. Discovering and knowing ourselves may, after all, become our purpose in life.

Conclusion

A T THE HEIGHT OF SUMMER, a colony of bees at full productive capacity numbers in the tens of thousands of individuals working as a single macroorganism across a radius of over eight kilometres. In the winter they adapt to a different role and pace, protecting the queen in an insulating mass not much bigger than a football. We have learnt how they grow and develop different skills. We have seen how they reproduce and make life or death decisions. We have observed how they communicate and how they can adapt the allocation of their resources in response to changes in the environment. I hope you have been curious and inspired to look again at these amazing insects.

I hope you have also been curious about the notion of bees and beekeeping as a fascinating metaphor for complex organisations, working life and leadership challenges today.

Through learning about the bees and what happens inside a hard-working colony, we hope you have gained a fresh perspective and taken twelve leadership lessons from inside a hive to think about and reflect on:

1. **Organisational Design.** Command-and-control models of hierarchical leadership are no longer fit for purpose in the majority of industries. If that's what you've based your career on until

now, it's time to think again. Be curious and open-minded about who you are and what kind of leader you want to be.

2. **Communications.** Let's all think harder about *how* we communicate, not just *what* we say. Messages must be received and understood. We need to be clear and consistent and to recognise emotions and 'antibodies' to change.

3. **Creativity.** New ideas and creativity come from an open mind and a fertile environment of connections, content and context. Keep sharing, building and collaborating to develop new approaches to ways of working.

4. **Productivity.** In the knowledge economy, your value will come from the *quality* of your output rather than the quantity. Chasing productivity and adding more tasks to your list won't bring you a real competitive advantage or make the impact you hope to achieve. Thinking harder, slowing down and pausing will. Let go of the old frameworks and embrace looking after yourself and your team.

5. **Learning.** Our human potential to keep learning is limitless. Keep an open mind to new roles and skills at work and in life. Like the bees, take on new and different roles and learn from people around you – those more senior and more junior, as well as those in other departments or industries.

6. **Decision-Making.** Decision-making is a key skill of leaders and organisations, but not all decisions are made equally or need the same approach. Build your awareness and skills of how a team needs to make decisions.

7. **Teamwork.** Teamwork is the key unit of success in organisations today. Leading a team is not a skill we are born with: it is developed. Therefore, do the work. Create a safe place for people to show up as who they are and be authentic at work.

Build connections. Build camaraderie. Build trust. Increasing our awareness and capabilities of how teams work as a unit, not just as a group of individuals, is a key skill. Be aware that not all teams are the same or need the same leadership style. By creating an environment that's psychologically safe and diverse and where everyone truly listens and is present, we can create an environment that is as bountiful as a beehive.

8. **Change and Diversity.** Organisations need to reflect the diversity of customers and society today. As a leader we need to be aware of our own biases and behaviours and build an environment that is inclusive and equitable.

9. **Using your Senses.** Stop, pause and think. Take more time to notice what is happening in a work setting and in life. Be more curious. Notice, observe and sense. Ask better questions. Listen more and talk less.

10. **Endings.** Life is a cycle of beginnings, middles and endings. Notice where your own energy is and that of your organisation. Pay more attention to these different phases and in particular how to close well. This applies to everything: meetings, projects and life!

11. **New Beginnings.** Let's all take time to reflect and learn what has gone well and where we need to pay more attention. How is our environment evolving? What skills and capabilities do we need for the next phase of our life and career?

12. **Purpose.** Why are we here? Take time to pause and reflect on the big questions. What do my family need right now and in the years to come? How can I contribute to society? What is fulfilling, and fun!? These are difficult questions and it's easy to not make time for them – working with a coach can help.

So in conclusion, let's all stop, pause and think harder. About the bees, about our work environment and our place in society as leaders, parents, role models and ambassadors. Are we fully present and connected to what is important? What is being communicated, verbally and nonverbally? Are we embracing those difficult conversations? Are we taking the necessary time to finish things as well as we start them, including our own careers? As we reach the end of one role and think about starting a new one, will that be more aligned with our purpose?

As my colleague Dave Kesby says, 'Everyone deserves to be led well'. Therefore, developing good leadership skills calls for a mindset shift and consistently exploring new ways of working. Curiosity is the catalyst of innovation, and a curious mindset will help you seek out challenges and new experiences that will broaden your horizons and help you to become a better leader – and individual. The only barrier is a self-defeating belief that none of that is possible.

Everything you know today you have learnt. Our human potential to keep learning is limitless, so if you're reading this book, you've already started the shift. And that's something to acknowledge and celebrate.

APPENDIX

The Last Bee by Brian Bilston

After the last ee
had uzzed its last uzz,

the irds and the utterflies
did what they could.

ut soon the fields lay are,
few flowers were left,

nature was roken,
and the planet ereft.

– RIAN ILSTON.

Ten Steps If You Are Inspired by the Bees

1. Teach children to respect bees, and not to be frightened by them or to swat them.
2. Consider the biodiversity of your garden or balcony.
3. Plant some wildflower seeds.
4. Consider locking up your lawnmower for 'No Mow May'.
5. Don't obsess about weeding – diversity is good!
6. Don't use pesticides on your garden – au natural is also beautiful.
7. If you find a swarm in your garden, contact your local beekeeping association.
8. Buy local honey and local organic food where you can.
9. Leave a local water source for bees to drink from.
10. If you are considering becoming a beekeeper, join a local society to learn how to do this.

Reflection for Leaders

If you are a leader or role model in an organisation, take some time to think:

- What has this book made you think about?
- What are you curious about?
- What challenged you?
- What conversations do you need to have?
- And with whom?
- As a result, what do you need to do differently?
- What one small step can you take today?
- Are there any books from our Further Reading list that interest you?

Book Club

One of my most interesting and thought-provoking events each month is meeting with my book club. We are a diverse group of people from across Europe with a shared interest in new ways of working and organisational and leadership development. We also frequently have wildly differing opinions, perspectives and experiences of reading the same texts. I love reading the chosen texts myself; however, I learn far more from hearing other views and additional comments.

If you would like to read this book as a book club, here are some questions you may want to pose to each other:

- What did you like about this book?
- What did you take from it?
- How well did the bee metaphor work for you?
- What did you find challenging?
- What did you not agree with or reject about the book?
- What are you curious to learn more about?
- Is there anything you will do differently or think about as a result of reading the book?
- Did you know male bees cannot feed themselves, or sting, or serve any other purpose than to mate, before being killed by the females!?
- Is there anything you'd like to ask the author?

Bees for Development

One important goal for this book project is to raise awareness and vital funds for the charity, Bees for Development. They work tirelessly to support communities in developing countries to make and sell honey as a sustainable business. Founded in 1993, Bees for Development is the global charity that makes life better with bees. They promote sustainable beekeeping to combat poverty, build resilient livelihoods and benefit biodiversity. Bees create economic incentive for people to care for them and for their food sources – which means that with every new beekeeper trained, Bees for Development creates an environmental champion. If conditions are good for bees, they are good for everything!

At Hive-Logic.com Coaching & Communications we are proud to be corporate sponsors of their work. Your purchase of this book will help us to raise awareness and to continue to fund some of their campaigns.

'I look forward to building on the solid foundation that founder Nicola Bradbear built. Our focus will continue to be teaching beekeeping to create sustainable and resilient livelihoods for vulnerable communities and by doing this, protect honey bees and biodiversity. The story of man's relationship with bees and beekeeping is a fascinating one and one that is essential to life on earth. Bees for Development have made a difference using beekeeping as a tool for sustainable development for over thirty years. This book represents a fresh look at beekeeping and I hope everyone who reads it takes away a greater insight to the life of bees and how we must support and protect them and give people the opportunity to work together with them in harmony.'

– MEGAN DENVER, CEO, Bees for Development

To learn more about Bees for Development or to make a donation, please use the QR code below or go to the website.

www.BeesForDevelopment.org

Further Reading

Below are a list of books that have inspired my work, and this book. I have also included books mentioned in the chapters, should you wish to add them to your reading list.

- *Honey: From Hive to Honeypot* by Sue Style
  This is the most poetic homage to bees I've read. Beautifully written and illustrated, it has been a great inspiration for this book. Thank you, dear Sue.
- *The Social Instinct: How Cooperation Shaped the World* by Nichola Raihani
  Do look for her work on YouTube – I saw her speak at the Royal Geographical Society and was blown away by her scientific mind and engaging storytelling.
- *Honeybee Democracy* by Thomas D. Seeley
  Quite the most remarkable work about swarming and bee decision-making. Professor Seeley is also a patron of the charity, Bees for Development.
- *In Praise of Bees: A Cabinet of Curiosities* by Elizabeth Birchall
  This is a fascinating insight into the whole world of beekeeping and honey production.
- *Collins Beekeeper's Bible: Bees, Honey, Recipes and Other Home Uses* by Philip McCabe, Richard A. Jones and Sharon Sweeney-Lynch

This is a beautiful and inspiring book. Great for a winter's night!

- *The Idle Beekeeper: The Low-Effort, Natural Way to Raise Bees* by Bill Anderson

This is a lovely and funny account of a beekeeper's year. Very accessible to read and so much to learn from.

- *Buzz: The Nature and Necessity of Bees* by Thor Hanson

A fascinating account of the natural history of the whole bee genus.

- *The Mind of a Bee* by Lars Chittka

Exploring the intelligence and cognitive abilities of bees.

About Organisational Development and New Ways of Working

- *Reinventing Organizations: A Guide to Creating Organizations Inspired by the Next Stage in Human Consciousness* by Frederic Laloux
- *Time to Think: Listening to Ignite the Human Mind* by Nancy Kline
- *Working Identity: Unconventional Strategies for Reinventing Your Career* by Herminia Ibarra
- *The Hive Mind at Work: Harnessing the Power of Group Intelligence to Create Meaningful and Lasting Change* by Siobhan McHale
- *The Insider's Guide to Culture Change: Creating a Workplace That Delivers, Grows, and Adapts* by Siobhan McHale
- *Four Thousand Weeks: Time Management for Mortals* by Oliver Burkeman
- *The 100-Year Life: Living and Working in an Age of Longevity* by Lynda Gratton and Andrew Scott
- *The Curious Advantage* by Paul Ashcroft, Simon Brown and Garrick Jones

Books by Guest Writers

- *Extra-Dependent Teams: Realising the Power of Similarity* by David Kesby
- *Clear Your Head to Get Ahead: The Antidote to Stress* by Martin Daubney
- *Scientifically Speaking: How to Speak About Your Research with Confidence and Clarity* by Jo Filshie Browning
- *The Fertile Void: Gestalt Coaching at Work* by John Leary-Joyce
- *Systemic Team Coaching* by John Leary-Joyce and Hilary Lines
- *The Leader's Fairytales* by Bernhard Sterchi

Suggested Reading from Guest Writers

- *Drive: The Surprising Truth About What Motivates Us* by Daniel Pink
- *Finite and Infinite Games: A Vision of Life as Play and Possibility* by James P. Carse
- *Give and Take: Why Helping Others Drives Our Success* by Adam Grant
- *Restoring Sanity: Practices to Awaken Generosity, Creativity, and Kindness in Ourselves and Our Organizations* by Margaret J. Wheatley
- *The Creative Act: A Way of Being* by Rick Rubin
- *Designing Your Life: How to Build a Well-Lived, Joyful Life* by Bill Burnett and Dave Evans
- *Feel-Good Productivity: How to Do More of What Matters to You* by Ali Abdaal
- *The Bees* by Laline Paull
- *Range: How Generalists Triumph in a Specialized World* by David Epstein
- *Peak Mind* by Amishi P. Jha
- *Thinking in Systems: A Primer* by Donella H. Meadows

Acknowledgements

Everything in life depends on teamwork.

I would like to acknowledge and say thank you to the following dear people who are a source of constant inspiration and support.

Thank you.

Bee buddy, Frank. A constant companion to share the highs and lows of beekeeping, the stings when it goes wrong and the positive buzz when we don't make so many mistakes. Thank you for everything, Frank.

The Alsace Syndicat d'Apiculture bee club. Thank you for making me feel so welcome. And for speaking more French than Alsacian dialect.

Benoit Dirring from my village, who provided so much bee keeping support in the early days. Merci Beaucoup, Benoit.

A special thank you goes to the dear members of my book club (you know who you are!). Each month you inspire me and have given me the confidence to try writing something myself.

The hive mind of the twelve guest writers – thank you for helping to lift this project to a greater level and for sharing your own experience and wisdom. And in particular to Jan Liska who prompted and poked, like the great coach he is, which was the genesis of this aspect of the book. Thank you everyone for your constant presence and support.

A special thank you must go to Corinna Cunningham and Kory Kirby, without whom this project would never have seen the light of day or have been such a fun process from beginning to end. Thank you to two very skilled, experienced and passionate professionals.

Finally, thank you to Susie, the queen to our hard-working family colony. Thank you for your tireless support of our whole family system that also allows these flights of fancy to take off.

Merci Beaucoup!

About the Guest Writers

Everything we do in life and at work is improved by partnering with other good people.

This book is not just about sharing my views; it's about creating a community towards shared thinking. So, the natural conclusion is, let's hear from more people and let's hear an additional or alternative view. As you read this book, you will discover that there is a great congruence between its message and how we work at Hive-Logic. Therefore, I asked the following twelve people to contribute to this book:

(Note: The opinions expressed by guest writers in this book are solely their own and do not reflect the views, opinions, or positions of their employers or any other affiliated organizations.)

Timm Urschinger

Timm is well known as the founder of LIVEsciences and co-founder of the Teal Around the World festival, which celebrates new ways of working and the work of Frederic Laloux's *Reinventing Organizations*. He is currently a partner at EY's Enterprise Transformation Practice in Switzerland.

Jo Filshie Browning

Jo Filshie Browning is one of the world's most experienced spokesperson trainers. She's a leading expert in the science of authority, and has trained top-level CEOs and thousands of professionals across the world to speak with impact and clarity. She is a TEDx speaker and author of the bestseller *Scientifically Speaking: How to Speak About Your Research with Confidence and Clarity.*

Ricardo Troiano

Ricardo is the co-founder of leadership advisory firm Concio.com, which works to support leaders and multinational organisations through change and transformation. He has lived on three continents and in four countries, starting as an engineer, then moving on to management consulting in learning, leadership, strategy and change practice, followed by a leading global industry role focused on change and organisational development.

Martin Daubney

Martin is a psychological coach based in Basel, Switzerland, and author of *Clear Your Head to Get Ahead.* Through his company, Inspire Coaching GmbH, he has worked with senior leaders and executives in global organisations to help them manage their stress, improving not only their performance (and mental well-being) but also the performance of their teams.

Katy Pountney

Katy is a human resources professional entering her third decade at a global pharmaceutical company based in Switzerland. Here, she enjoys the challenge of regularly reinventing organisations, teams and individuals, and not least her own contributions. Before that, having trained as a tax consultant, she worked as an HR consultant in the UK and Czech Republic.

Bernhard Sterchi

Bernhard has been called a thought sorter and player of Tetris with ideas. As managing partner of Palladio Trusted Advisers, he works as trainer, coach and consultant. He is the author of *The Leader's Fairytales* and *Oblique Strategies for Leaders*, and creator of the Peerview App.

Dave Kesby

Dave is an experienced executive and team coach who authored *Extra-Dependent Teams: Realising the Power of Similarity*. He is the founder of Organisational Coaching Hub, which provides coaching capabilities to organisations, teams and individuals. He is driven by his purpose that 'Everyone deserves to be led well'.

Jacqueline Rosenberg

Jacqueline is an organisation development, change and inclusion leader with a long career in the life sciences sector. She also has significant experience in market research, policy and consulting across the private, public and non-profit sectors. She is a behavioural scientist with a PhD in Health Behaviour Change.

Suzanne Lee

Suzanne is the head of Global Talent, Learning and Organisation Development for a global medical device company. She is committed to continuous learning and is currently completing her PhD in Organisational Change, focusing on the dynamics of intimacy and power within growing organisations.

John Leary-Joyce

John is the author of The Fertile Void: Gestalt Coaching at Work and Systemic Team Coaching. He was co-founder of the Gestalt Centre

London in 1979 and founder of the Academy of Executive Coaching, AoEC.com, in 1999. He combines his individual/team coaching, supervision and training with a passion for dancing Argentine tango – always in the moment.

Guy Dickinson

Guy is a behavioural scientist and has a long career in Pharma and consulting to support behavioural change, capability building, strategy and innovation. He has a specific interest in digital transformation, AI and the future of work. He was most recently head of Employee Experience at Novartis.

Jan Liska

Jan has been creating products, brands and services setting new standards for beauty, well-being, health and care at L'Oréal, Shiseido and Sanofi. As a global innovator, strategist, behaviour researcher and executive coach, Jan opens new possibilities for people to live the best version of their lives, with self-confidence, curiosity and joy.

About the Author

Philip Atkinson is based in Alsace, France, and is the founder of Hive-Logic.com Coaching & Communications with offices in Basel, Switzerland and London, UK. Philip is a leadership team expert and organisational coach and shares his wisdom of his two great passions together in one volume. As a beekeeper, Philip loves to spend the summer tending to and observing his precious bees and spending the winter learning, reading and writing about them. Throughout the whole year, Philip supports leadership teams and leaders worldwide to grow and develop. His Hive-Logic company is run like a collaborative beehive, and they support senior leaders and teams at multinational organisations to perform at their best with coaching, training and facilitation. Learn more about their work at Hive-Logic.com. Philip has four children who help with the beekeeping. He is therefore no stranger to stinging feedback.